How to Teach Adults

Plan Your Class.
Teach Your Students.
Change the World.

EXPANDED EDITION

Dan Spalding

JB JOSSEY-BASS™
A Wiley Brand

Published by Jossey-Bass
A Wiley Brand
One Montgomery Street, Suite 1200, San Francisco, CA 94104-4594—www.josseybass.com

Jossey-Bass books and products are available through most bookstores. To contact Jossey-Bass
directly call our Customer Care Department within the U.S. at 800-956-7739, outside the U.S.
at 317-572-3986, or fax 317-572-4002.

Wiley publishes in a variety of print and electronic formats and by print-on-demand. Some
material included with standard print versions of this book may not be included in e-books or
in print-on-demand. If this book refers to media such as a CD or DVD that is not included in
the version you purchased, you may download this material at http://booksupport.wiley.com.
For more information about Wiley products, visit www.wiley.com.

*Library of Congress Cataloging-in-Publication Data has been applied for and is on file with the
Library of Congress.*
    ISBN 978-1-118-84136-5 (cloth)
    ISBN 978-1-118-84137-2 (ebk)
    ISBN 978-1-118-84128-0 (ebk)

Printed in the United States of America
FIRST EDITION

PB Printing   10 9 8 7 6 5 4 3 2

THE JOSSEY-BASS HIGHER AND ADULT EDUCATION SERIES

So Glenn Chilberg

CONTENTS

To my parents, my first and best teachers.

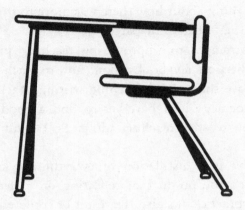

WHY I WROTE THIS BOOK

And why you should read it.

You've had bad teachers before. You had the teacher who lectured in a monotone the entire class. You had the teacher whose answers to your questions confused instead of clarified. You had teachers who wasted your time with busywork, who tested you on things never covered in class, and who gave you grades that bore no relationship to what you put into the course or got out of it.

Maybe you've been that teacher. Maybe you gave a workshop that put your colleagues to sleep. Maybe you taught a course that left you frustrated at the end of each class period. Maybe, right now, you're going through the motions of being a teacher, making your students happy but not teaching them half as much as they ought to be learning. Maybe your fear of failure is keeping you away from teaching in the first place.

Teaching adults is hard. When I started, I didn't think you needed any special skills to do it. Then, one day about a month into my first semester, every single one of my students went home during the break. An hour in a classroom all by myself gave me a lot of time to think about how there was more to this "teaching adults" thing than I had anticipated.

In my attempts to improve my teaching practice, I've learned that there are few books about how to teach adults, and all of them have their niche: teaching writing, teaching tennis, teaching democracy . . . I have yet to find a good book that shows you how to start teaching adults. So I spent three years writing one.

This book is a distillation of everything I know about the subject. It's the product of reflecting on a decade of my own teaching practice. It's also the result of conferences, professional development workshops, and collaborations with other teachers. It even has the best tips and insights from all those specialized teaching books I read. I believe that *How to Teach Adults* is the first and best book for anyone who cares about the subject. It's a concentrated reference you'll come back to again and again.

If you give workshops, this book will help you prepare and present them better. If you're thinking about making a career in adult education, this book will convince you that it's the best job in the world. If you're a beginning teacher in search of some guidance, this book will give you concrete advice you can use to build your career for the long haul. And if you're a veteran instructor looking for something you can use tomorrow, go directly to Chapter 6, How to Run Your Class and Chapter 7, How to Present Information. You can read this book from beginning to end or skip around to find exactly what you need.

How to Teach Adults was written for athletic coaches, yoga instructors, spiritual leaders, and drill sergeants, in addition to the math professors and English as a Second Language instructors we usually think of as adult educators. Whoever you are, I want to help you become the person you want to be. That's what adult education is all about.

TEACH YOURSELF HOW TO TEACH

You are your own first student.

My name is Dan Spalding, and I'm a teacher. I've taught English as a Second Language (ESL) for over ten years to immigrants in Oakland, and I've facilitated "Know Your Rights" workshops for thousands of activists around the country.

As a student, I've studied in traditional public and private institutions, including earning my BA at a small private liberal arts college and my MA in Teaching English to Speakers of Other Languages (TESOL) at a big state university. I've also trained at a dojo where I've reached black belt rank in jujitsu and Aikido. I got some of the best instruction of my life there.

I started this book with a question. What should I have known when I first started teaching? The first answer is that I should have known how much I'd have to teach myself how to teach.

I'm going to help you cheat. You'll still have to teach yourself, but I'm going to give you everything you need to get that process started as efficiently and effectively as possible.

TEACHING IS THE BEST JOB IN THE WORLD

We help make people free.

In 1880s Poland, Marie Curie was a bright young high school graduate who was excluded from the state universities, which only served male students. She instead attended "the flying university," an underground coeducational network created by women. Teachers organized small classes in their homes, moving constantly to avoid the authorities. They even had a secret library!

Curie went on to discover radiation with her husband, with whom she shared the 1903 Nobel Prize in Physics; in 1911 she won the Chemistry Nobel on her own. Curie was the first woman to win a Nobel Prize, the first person to win two Nobel Prizes, and is still the only laureate in two different sciences.

Forty-four years later, a secretary for the Montgomery NAACP named Rosa Parks traveled to Tennessee to study civil disobedience. She spent two weeks at the Highlander Folk School, a small grassroots institution that trained generations of activists how to organize against the problems facing their communities. It's where the civil rights movement learned "We Shall Not Be Moved" from the labor movement.

Weeks after leaving Highlander, Rosa Parks launched the Montgomery Bus Boycott. Mainstream history books say she was just tired the day she refused to move to the back of the bus, but in her words, "No, the only tired I was, was tired of giving in." The facilitators at Highlander, as well as the other civil rights organizers who were part of that same training, gave her the skills and self-confidence to change history. Highlander continued to train generations of organizers, despite getting branded a Communist training camp, having its property confiscated by the state of Tennessee, and being forced to relocate.

The theme, to me, is that while institutions keep people in line (state-run universities in Poland and Jim Crow in the South), teachers help make people free. No matter what you teach, when you foster critical thinking, collaboration, and hard work in the classroom, you not only employ best teaching practices, you help make your students—and everyone else—a little more free.

So work hard. You may be teaching the next Marie Curie or Rosa Parks right now.

Note: *I talk more about the big picture role of teachers in Chapter 10, The Future of Education.*

TEACHING GROWNUPS IS MORE FUN THAN TEACHING KIDS

I'll get no love from K–12 teachers for saying this.

Besides the inspiration, there's one big reason to choose teaching adults over kids. Adults students are more fun. Adults make better conversation, bring more life experience, and ultimately have more to give to each other and to you.

My students have told me where you can buy a fake Social Security card in Oakland and what life is like in a refugee camp in Thailand. They've told me about underground clubs and high school race riots. My adults students have taught me more about my city and the rest of the world than I could have learned in a hundred lifetimes.

Story: I was teaching my class about the 1912 Bread and Roses Strike when one of my students, an older, handsome Cuban immigrant of African descent, told us about labor protests in Japanese factories after World War II. Rather than strike, workers actually sped up the production line. This generated a surplus of finished goods that was costly to warehouse and embarrassing for plant managers to explain to their superiors. Being of Japanese descent myself, I appreciated how intensely Japanese this mode of protest was. The student mentioned that he learned about this in Moscow, where he trained to be an air force radar technician for the Cuban military.

To recap, a Cuban veteran taught a room full of immigrants in America the Japanese labor history that he studied in Russia. In what K–12 class would this have happened?

ACKNOWLEDGMENTS

Everyone who has helped me become a better teacher has helped me write this book, and vice versa. First, I am indebted to Bob Wells, who may have lied when he told me that teaching English to adults was so easy it was "a scam," but made up for it by mentoring me those first painful months. My ESL practice was further nurtured by my colleagues at Oakland Adult and Career Education, particularly Barbara Knox and Don Curtis. Thanks for those safe(r) bike rides home. I am also grateful for the efforts of my fellow unionists in the American Federation of Teachers; no one fought harder to preserve free adult education in Oakland.

I am indebted to my good friends at Suigetsukan dojo, especially Mike, Gina, Jorin, Rebecca, and the other sensei who taught me over the years. Suigetsukan is an embodiment of what adult education should be: high quality, pay what you can, judgment free, and kick ass.

At the beginning of my career, Art Ellison, of the New Hampshire Bureau of Adult Education, sent me a care package of adult ed books without even knowing me—including *Unearthing Seeds of Fire*, which introduced me to the Highlander Center. He was also kind enough to look at the earliest drafts of this book. Thanks for reminding me not to be so cynical, Art.

I am indebted to my professors at Oberlin College, in particular politics profs Eve Sandberg, Ron Kahn, and Chris Howell, the latter of whom has given me a continuing education in labor studies long after my classes with him were over.

I am thankful to the instructors in my San Francisco State University MA program, particularly Drs. Barry Taylor, David Olsher, and Troi Carleton. Thanks also to my colleagues in the Laney College ESL department, particularly Steve Zetlan and Sonja Franeta, who helped get me up to speed. And I learned much from my former mentee teachers Levana Saxon and Lisa Gonzalvez, who have since eclipsed me in the teaching profession. Please don't forget your old friend Dan.

More recently, I am grateful to my many good friends at Intrax, particularly Mike Missiaen for his close reading of my first final draft. I am grateful for Mark Trushkowsky's edits to an early draft; you make criticism feel like a hug, Mark. Thanks to all my fabulous readers, particularly Natalie Mottley, Lee Worden, Christopher Hein, Levana Saxon (again), Sarah Koster, Meegan Rivera, Eve Beals, Heather Frank, and Zoe Madden-Wood. Much of my inspiration to keep teaching comes from Jesse Robinson, who saw this "book" when it was an uncategorized list of topic sentences. You're my teacher hero, Jesse.

A quick shout-out to the baristas at Four Barrel, Blue Bottle, Rodger's, and Stanza, in whose cafés this book was mostly written. Props to Modern Times, The Harvard Bookstore, and The Strand, where I made many a happy teaching book discovery. There's still no substitute for a good bookstore.

Huge thanks to my Kickstarter backers, who generously supported the early version of this project. Your names appear at the end of these acknowledgments. *How to Teach Adults* wouldn't be half as beautiful without your help. Thanks also to Dan Roam, whose book *Back of the Napkin* helped me sketch the images which my good friends Sabiha Basrai and Ria at Design Action Collective turned into the beautiful diagrams and illustrations here—with the exception of Clifford Harper's fabulous woodblock print illustration at the beginning of Chapter 10.

Thank you to Larry Daloz, who wrote encouraging e-mails and a fantastic book; *Mentor* is a mitzvah to everyone who teaches adults. Thanks as well to my new editor, David Brightman, whose unflagging support and endless supply of teaching books were key to this one coming together. Thank you to Ramsey at PM Press for some last-minute advice, and thank you to my lawyer, Ria Julien, for looking out for me.

Thank you to the hundreds of students I've taught since 2002. Bumping into y'all in the streets of Oakland is one of my favorite things about being alive.

And I am most grateful for the support of my wife, Christy Tennery, without whom, what's the point?

THANK YOU, KICKSTARTER BACKERS

I'd like to extend a special shout-out to my Kickstarter supporters. Without you this book would not have been possible. Thank you.

Adam Jasiura
Adam Tannir
Alexandre Krstic
Amanda Hogan
Andrew McKay
Angel Georgiev
Anthony Watts
Ash Lauth
Ashlee Albies
Audrey
Audrey Watters
Becca Barnes
Benjamin Bangsberg
Benjamin Lebsanft

Bess Williamson
Big Jeff
Bill Meador
Bill Sides
Bo Davis
Brent Sieling
Brian E Munroe
Briana & Connor Cavanaugh
Brihannala Morgan
Brooks Graham
Bryan Castañeda
Bryan Wehrli
C. Violeta Hernandez
Calvin Lim

Cash Durrett

Chris Ainsworth

Chris G.

Chris Howell

Chris Lambert

Christian Buggedei

Christy Tennery

Clare Marie Myers

Connie Lamborn

Dan Gregor

Dan Marshall

Dan Pierce

Daragh Hayes

Dave Hinman

David Eaman

David Large

David McConeghy

David Otaguro

Debora Gordon

Deborah Lea Smith

Delia Turner

Diana Pei Wu

Diane E. Main

Diane McEachern

Dmitry Lavrov

Don Graham

Donielle Buie

Draco Whitefire

Edward

Elizabeth McKinstry

Elizabeth Mount

Emerald Betts

Emily Harris

Emily Van Engel

Eric Romano

Erika Tastrophe

Esther Wojcicki

Eva Jo

Faffs T. Jackalinski

Fereshteh Toosi

Frank Quattro

Gabriel Bianchi

Gaylynne Hudson

Gerard Cronin

Giel van Schijndel

Glenn Reker

Greg Gerrand

Hannah Merriman

Heather James

Heather Mooney

Henry C. Schmitt

hugh smith

Ian Byrd

Irina Ceric

J Roth

Jacobus Kats

Jacqueline Bondurant

James Collins

Jan Tiedemann

Jeanean Slamen

Jemima Talbot

Jene

Jennifer Borchardt

Jeremy S. Kirkwood

Jesse Chenven

Jessica Rigby

Joanna M. R.

Joanna Solins

Joe Shaffer

Joel Friesen

Jonathan Edmonds

Josh RC

Joshua James

JPR

Julian G.

Julien Goodwin

Kara T. Stenberg

Kathy Kohut

Katie Osborn

Keith Ikeda-Barry

Kenneth B. Haase

Kiele

Kim Giacalone

Kimlin and Kirk

Kitt Hodsden

Koha Yoga

Larry Rosenstein

Larry Zieminski

Lauren Currie Lewis

Law Offices of Carpenter and
    Mayfield

Leah Rorvig

Lee Worden

Linda

Lindsay Knisely

Lindsay Simon

Liz Blair

Lutz F. Krebs

Marena Kehl

Margaret Sheridan

Margot Brennan

Mari Cohen

Mark Jason Trushkowsky

Marshall Haker

Martin Macias, Jr.

Matt Leonard

Maurice C. Cherry

Maya Valladares

Megan Lehman

Melanie D. Viramontes

Melo Kalemkeridis

Meredith R. Dearborn

Michael Bungay Stanier

Michael Lawson

Michael Townsley

Michal Minecki

Mike B. Fisher

Mike Kabakoff

Mike Missiaen

Mike Stevenson

Morgan

Myka

Neal Melton

Neil Sakamoto

Nico Veenkamp

nicole harkin

Noppasorn Sakornpanish

Nora Sawyer

Olivia Wilkins

Oz Raisler Cohn

Pansycow

Pat Miles

Patrick A. Smith
Paul Jonusaitis
Perry Gaidurgis
Peter Weber
Rabbi Andrew M. Horowitz
Raymond Pompon
Rebecca Solnit
Rebecca Wolfinger
Rich Peterson
Rob Yanagida
Robert C. Bennett
Robyn
Rod Fage
Ross Smith
Sam Larson
Sarah
Scott David Edwards
Sean James
Sharon Smith
shawn looker
Shira
Song Kim

Stefan Ohrmann
Stephen Keaveny
Steve Mandamadiotis
Susan Sylvesster
Theron Trowbridge
Thomas E. Booker
Thomas M. Johnson
Tim Leahy
Tom
Tom Croucher
Tom Gromak
Tracy LeRoy
Trevor Mcpherson
Vanessa Sacks
Vernon White
Wm. Bruce Davis
Wong Kum Kit
Yolanda C. Denny
Yvonne Woo
Zara Zimbardo
Zoe Madden-Wood

ABOUT THE AUTHOR

Dan Spalding began facilitating workshops for activists after participating in the 1999 Seattle WTO protests. The following year he cofounded the Midnight Special Law Collective, a nonprofit dedicated to teaching people their rights and providing legal support for those protesting for social justice. In the following decade he helped train thousands of peace activists, undocumented youth fighting for US citizenship, and high school students who wanted to know their rights when harassed by the police. He also wrote curriculum around activist trainings, trainer-trainings, and how to set up a legal office for a protest.

Dan started teaching English as a Second Language in 2002 in Oakland, California. He first taught beginning English to Chinese immigrants before moving on to teach intermediate-level English to a mixed group of students from around the world. He later taught at the workforce development program at Laney Community College in Oakland before developing online curriculum for a number of Web start-ups in San Francisco.

Dan received a BA in politics from Oberlin College, an MA in teaching English at San Francisco State University, and black belts in jujitsu and Aikido from Suigetsukan dojo. Dan lives with his wife, Christy Tennery, in the Bay Area, where you can often find him reading, bicycling, drinking coffee, and making trouble. *How to Teach Adults* is his first book. To find out more, go to www .teachrdan.com. You can reach him at teachrdan@gmail.com.

How to
Teach Adults

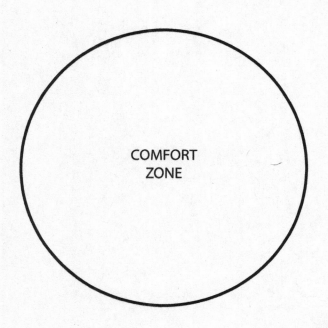

COMFORT
ZONE

BE HERE

CHAPTER 1

Foundations of Teaching

SAFETY FIRST, DISCOMFORT SECOND

Students can't learn when they're comfortable.

We humans instinctively stay in our comfort zone—a literal and metaphorical space where everything is familiar and easy.[1] When it comes to learning, students' comfort zone is receiving the information they're used to in the formats they're used to, engaging it how they're used to at the pace that they're used to.

It's hard to get yourself out of your own comfort zone. That's one reason people take classes—to get information they're not used to (new facts, new perspectives), in formats they're not used to (lectures, academic writing), engaging it in new ways (group activities, portfolio projects) at a faster (or more deliberate) pace. Whether they know it or not, students come to you because they've hit the limit of what they can learn in their comfort zone.

This leads me to conclude that, in order to maximize student learning, teachers must make students uncomfortable. Your job is to create a thoughtful, supportive environment that invites (or forces) students to attempt new challenges and learn from them. Reward risk taking, even if students are not immediately successful, because those risks help students get out of their comfort zone and break through old boundaries.

Get students into the discomfort zone as much as possible. That's where learning lives. (For tips on teaching this concept on the first day of class, see Chapter 4, "Teach the discomfort zone.")

What you should not do is push students into their alarm zone. This is where students feel unsafe and shut down. Watch out for when students grow silent or get angry. Even if they're not visibly distraught, they may be in their alarm zone. Forcing a student to do a presentation in front of the class, which he stammers through, red-faced, before rushing out the door, is an example of a student likely pushed into their alarm zone. (See Figure 1.1.)

When you see students get into their alarm zone, immediately change or end what you're doing. Transition to an activity they're familiar with, especially a solo reflection process like journal writing. You can use this as an opportunity for students to think about what they got out of the activity or to debrief what was so difficult about it.

On the other hand, don't panic if students occasionally get irritated or frustrated. An emotional response is the best indication that students are in their discomfort zone. The better you get to know your students, the easier it will be to distinguish discomfort from alarm.

When students succeed in their discomfort zone, they expand their comfort zone forever. The same goes for teachers, too.

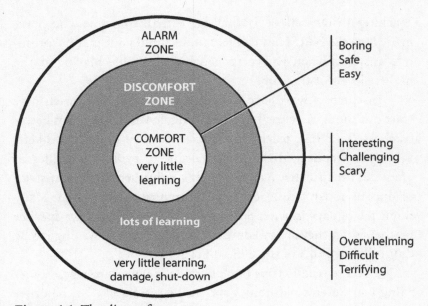

Figure 1.1 The discomfort zone
Source: Adapted with permission from Training for Change, 2012.

> **Hint:** *Some students are in their discomfort zone just by coming to class. If so, build trust to get them into their comfort zone before pushing them out of it again. (See Chapter 6, "Build trust to maximize learning.")*

BEING AN EXPERT DOESN'T MAKE YOU A GOOD TEACHER

Struggling with a subject helps you teach it.

Just being good at something doesn't qualify you to teach it. A Super Bowl–winning quarterback may actually have more trouble coaching a high school football team than someone who never made it to the NFL. How can you understand your players' primitive mistakes when you've spent your whole life playing at the highest levels of the game?

Instructors who have struggled with what they teach may start out more insecure, but their struggle will make them better teachers. Take ESL teachers who aren't native English speakers. Without exception, they are better able to explain the rules of grammar because they had to painstakingly learn them all, instead of unconsciously acquiring English grammar as children. Many English language learners are more inspired by nonnative-speaker teachers than they are by some sucker who just knows English by dint of being born in the United States.

If you're reading this book because you want to teach something you weren't naturally good at, be reassured. On the other hand, if you want to teach something at which you are gifted, know that, in some ways, your struggle is just beginning.

Note: *Struggling with your field of study also deepens your compassion for your students.*

TRY TO SEE FROM THE STUDENT'S PERSPECTIVE

Understand how students don't understand.

My first assumption about teaching was that it meant transmitting information to students. I was an expert in the English language and my job was to upload that expertise to my class. It was a while before I could articulate how that wasn't the case. I gradually realized that my job was to maximize learning, which is what goes on within the student. My focus switched from pouring information out of myself to creating situations that facilitated students building their own knowledge.

In order to maximize learning, you must be able to see from the student's perspective. Your job is to understand every one of your students so that you can create activities that maximize each student's ability to learn what you have to teach.

The best use of my own English language expertise wasn't to simply explain vocabulary and grammar. I needed to gauge students' ability at any given task, anticipate mistakes they were likely to make, and create activities to maximize their ability to learn new material. For example, if I was teaching the word "too," it wasn't enough to explain the textbook definition of "an excess of, used before quantity words like 'much' or 'many.'" I needed to know that students often use "too" interchangeably with "so," which explains why a Muslim student once told me, "There are too many Muslims in America!"

The ability to imagine is one of your most important teaching skills. You must imagine how students will engage your activities, your assignments, and your subject as a whole. When students make mistakes, don't just correct them. Examine those mistakes to figure out how your students think about what you teach. In so doing, you will improve your understanding of each student's perspective, which will do wonders for your teaching.

Go beyond academics and imagine the entire student experience. Students have to negotiate their classes, the school bureaucracy, their interactions with other students, as well as their work and family lives. It puts your latest homework assignment in perspective.

> **Note:** *The "student's" perspective in the title isn't a typo. My intention is to try to see things the way each individual student does, and to tailor my class to each student's needs.*

FIND OUT WHERE STUDENTS ARE ON THEIR JOURNEYS

Models of adult development can help you understand your students.

We're supposed to see our students as individuals. Each has goals and challenges unique to that student alone. At the same time, there is a lifelong journey common to us all. Seeing where each student is on that journey helps us understand where to help him or her go next.

Laurent Daloz introduced me to several powerful theories of adult learner development in his classic book *Mentor.* The one I found most compelling was created by William Perry, a professor at the Harvard Graduate School of Education.

After analyzing data collected on fifteen years of Harvard undergraduates, Perry theorized a linear path of adult learner development. It begins with freshmen college students expecting professors to simply pour knowledge into them. At this stage only a higher authority can tell the students what the truth is, and distinguish for them right from wrong. Lesser authorities—such as books, other students, or the students' own insights—offer nothing of value.

A year or two later, after exposure to many contradictory facts and perspectives—and after changing their own convictions a few times—these students refuse to take sides on any issue.

Why bother when they (or the experts) will inevitably change their mind? "What's the right answer?" is replaced by "It's all relative, man."

Senior year brings a final change. After countless lectures exploring various theories; classroom (and late-night) discussions showing how reasonable people can draw different conclusions from the same information; and term papers which make the students reflect on their beliefs, and then reflect on those reflections; the students learn to consciously use logical reasoning and personal conviction to construct a worldview they are willing to commit to.

Perry's model students emerge from their four-year cocoon with the twin truths of a liberal education: there are always multiple legitimate perspectives, and you must choose the one truest to you. The student graduates more open to new truths but better able to discern falsehood. (To quote Professor Andrew Delbanco, "we might say that the most important thing one can acquire in college is a well-functioning bullshit meter" [2012, 29]).

William Perry depicts a magic ladder transporting adult learners from credulity to apathy to self-mastery. To his credit, Perry was also fond of saying, "the first characteristic of any theory is that it is wrong in any particular case." (Daloz, 2012, 77). Humans are clearly more complex than any single model can account for.

I am only now, after ten years of teaching, beginning to apply these models of adult learner development to my students. No one expects you to master these theories before you begin your career. Having said that, by understanding the individual path each student walks and the intellectual approaches that map our many paths, your ability to teach will improve dramatically. For instance, when a student insists on knowing the one right answer, and thinks that you're hiding it when you insist there isn't one!

YOUR JOB IS TO HELP STUDENTS LEARN

I'm putting on my serious face for this one.

We all bring romantic misunderstandings about teaching into the classroom. These notions diminish us, our students, and our teaching practice.

Let's begin by discussing what teaching is not. Teaching is not about your feeling of satisfaction—although your feelings are an integral part of you and your practice. Teaching is not about students liking you, or loving you, or fearing you.

You teach to help your students learn. The degree to which they do so is the best measure of your success. If you focus on student learning, you won't waste time worrying about whether you're funny or creative enough, things you have little control over anyway. And if you're already funny and creative, focusing on learning will ensure that you go beyond entertaining your students.

To help students learn, you often have to teach them study skills: how to work in a group, study effectively, practice new skills at home, and so on. Ideally, these skills translate to life outside the classroom: how to work in a team, conduct research, make presentations, and so forth.

You may also need to teach "metaskills," abstract skills that govern a range of concrete ones. The ability to deliberately choose how best to prepare for a quiz (like deciding between creating flash cards or forming a study group) is one example of a metaskill. Metaskills are inherently more difficult to teach but give students more agency as workers or learners.

Whatever you do, spend as little time as possible on skills unique to your institution—or your class: how to take a blue book exam, post to your class blog, and so on. There's no opportunity for transfer with those skills.

8

Note: You teach the way you learn. If you learn best by reading, you're likely to give your students too much reading. If you learn best by doing, you may not put enough big-picture perspective into your curriculum. Be aware of this bias. Your job is to teach every student, not just those who learn the same way you do.

YOU TEACH THE WHOLE STUDENT, TOO

There is no such thing as only teaching information.

Adult education today focuses almost entirely on job skills. I respect the hell out of that. Students deserve to learn what they want, and teaching a specific skill—whether it's architectural drawing or cooking a soufflé—is a worthwhile goal.

And yet. Most of us teach because we believe that education can change our students and the world. This has little to do with job skills; instead, it's about helping people live more empowered and meaningful lives.

I believe there are opportunities to teach content and empowerment at the same time. When I taught workplace communication to a class of mostly black and Latino welding students, I created role plays where they had to negotiate with their boss to fix a dangerous workplace situation. For example, the class would read an accident report where a worker was killed when a metal I-beam fell onto him because it was standing upright on uneven ground. Then a student would role-play asking the boss (another student) to use a crane to move an unsafe beam. The whole class watched and gave the "worker" tips on how to be more persuasive.

You could say I was just teaching another job skill. Indeed, few things can delay construction more than a worksite injury.

But there are plenty of bosses who'd just as soon not have their workers know how to bargain with them.

The time spent on that role play could have just as well been spent memorizing Ohm's Law or some other esoterica. But I wanted my students to have more power in their lives. As was clear by the end of the role play, the skills you use to negotiate with your boss—active listening, logical reasoning, taking a stand—could be used just as well with authorities in government or in our families. The goal was not simply to make my students better worker bees but to give them more personal agency.

Some adult learners, depending on where they are on their journey, may resist your efforts to teach such abstract skills. But perhaps the highest art of teaching is finding the balance between promoting personal growth and teaching the concrete skills I implored you to focus on in the previous section.

TEACH FOR TRANSFER

Not for tests.

Few things in teaching are as thorny as transfer. Perhaps that's why it's so rarely discussed. Basically, transfer is the ability to apply classroom learning out in the real world. The conundrum is that it's hard to measure in the classroom what students can do outside the classroom.

True learning is when students incorporate what you teach into who they are. There are two challenges here. The obvious one is that students might not get what you're teaching. We'll talk a lot about that in the rest of the book. The less obvious challenge is that some students—particularly "good" ones—can memorize the material without being able to apply it. They are able to create a self-contained mental universe where they store and manipulate the information you provide without ever letting it touch who they are. These are the students who can give you every form of a thousand Spanish verbs without being able to buy a soda in a Mexican corner store. They're the tennis players who can hit a good forehand in practice but always smash the ball in a match.

Another reason it's hard to teach "good" students is because they're expert in giving false signals. They do all their homework and perform well on tests without actually learning anything. Contrast that to "bad" students who don't even come up with an excuse for why they didn't do their homework. That's one reason it can be easier to judge transfer in bad students than in good ones. They won't fake it to make you happy. (Their candor can be refreshing.)

American culture assumes that tests measure transfer, but the facts don't bear that out. A 1999 study published by the University of Michigan Law School showed that performance on the Law School Admissions Test (LSAT) did nothing to predict professional earnings or job satisfaction.[2] (They did find a negative correlation between high grades and test scores and community service.) More generally, a 1984 study found no correlation between grades in school and future earnings or job satisfaction. Follow-up studies have varied slightly without contradicting it.[3]

Transfer is why teachers hate teaching to the test. Good teachers prepare students for life beyond the classroom. Even if we can never measure how successful we are.

CULTIVATE INTRINSIC MOTIVATION

> *"If you want to build a ship, don't drum up the men to gather wood, divide the work and give orders. Instead, teach them to yearn for the vast and endless sea."*
>
> —Antoine de Saint-Exupéry, Author of *The Little Prince*[4]

Many adult students go back to school due to extrinsic motivation—the pursuit of external reward. There's nothing wrong with that. Extrinsic motivations—like wanting to earn more money—have pushed countless students out of their comfort zone.

Other adult students return to school due to intrinsic motivation: because they love the subject or they simply love to learn. Extrinsic and intrinsic motivations are both legitimate. But as far back as 1968, Malcolm Knowles theorized that adult learners inspired by intrinsic motivation learn better (Merriam, Caffarella, and Baumgartner, 2007, 84). Although that has been contested, no one denies that intrinsic motivation is powerful.

I think that adult educators are biased toward extrinsic motivation. We constantly tell students how what we teach will help them make more money or otherwise be more successful. So try to foster intrinsic motivation, too. Teach students to love the subject by showing how it has helped make you a better person. (See Chapter 8, "Disclose thoughtfully.") Or build a love of learning itself by explaining how long periods of apparent stagnation are followed by short bursts of intense progress. (See Chapter 3, "Progress is uneven; take advantage of this.")

Intrinsic motivation is powerful. Help students cultivate theirs so they can sail the seas of autonomous learning.

LEARNING IS HARD WORK

That work can be as much emotional as it is intellectual.

I believe the primary challenge to transfer is emotional. Unless you teach in prison, whatever your students are doing in life is working for them. They're functional and comfortable—and that means they're comfortable with their own limits.

A big part of teaching is making students' limits clear to them, and convincing them that they can break through those limits. This can be scary. The student with a thousand Spanish verbs is great at memorizing vocab—and terrified to actually speak Spanish. He's more likely to keep learning new verbs than to start working on his oral fluency, even if that's what he really needs. Why mess with success? The tennis player with the killer backhand is able to win many of her matches. Why would she replace her most powerful tool with something inferior?

You're basically telling people to abandon what they know just to deliberately fail at something new. And failing at a task—especially one central to your identity—feels like being a failure. Failing in front of your peers, some of whom may intimidate you, some of whom you may hold in contempt, is even more difficult.

A big part of teaching is making students do the lower-level stuff that they need, rather than the harder, more advanced stuff they think they need. People primarily judge their skill level (and self-worth) by the most extreme thing they're capable of doing. The tennis player may think she needs to add a few miles per hour to her overhead smash. But what she actually needs is to use her forehand every match. Your job is to convince her that this isn't a punishment, or a demotion, but what she needs most to improve.

If students don't work hard, intellectually and emotionally, they won't learn. You can be a cheerleader or a drill sergeant, but either way you need to motivate students to do that hard work. Especially when the work is hard because it's easier.

Note: *Students will never take an assignment more seriously than the teacher does. Show students that you're working hard and they'll work hard, too.*

ADULT EDUCATION HAS A POSSE

Which is to say it has a rich intellectual tradition.

Most of us happily stumble into adult education. Without the years of training required of other professions, we may never learn about the different intellectual traditions which inform the practice of adult education today.

Modern approaches to adult education in the United States begin with John Dewey. A philosopher, educator, and public intellectual, Dewey (1859–1952) pioneered the notion that student learning had to be grounded in experience, rather than rote memorization. Dewey's model teacher would structure classes so that students had new experiences—in math, or science, or literature—that meaningfully connected to their existing life experience. This was important for children, but even more so for adults, who brought more life experience to the classroom.

Dewey believed the ultimate goal of education was to make people open to more learning, to fresh ideas, and to better making sense of them. Or, as Dewey put it, "No experience is educative that does not tend both to knowledge of more facts and entertaining of more ideas and to a better, a more orderly, arrangement of them" (1938/1997, 82).

Dewey is the granddaddy of American adult education. Figures like Myles Horton, cofounder of the legendary Highlander School, made social change central to experiential education—and vice versa. When black and white antisegregation activists from the South went to train at Highlander, they didn't get lectured on the importance of desegregated living. Highlander simply assigned black and white attendees to share rooms for the week. This would invariably be their first experience living on equal terms with the "other" race (Friend, 1957).

14

Brazilian radical educator Paulo Freire also grounded education in students' life experience. He taught illiterate rural laborers how to read and write with curriculum based on the exploitation in their lives—part of a process he called "conscientization." (It sounds better in Portuguese.) At the same time, he identified how teachers could be agents of oppression as well as liberation, by teaching students simply to be more efficient exploited workers, rather than to fight against their exploitation. This undermined Dewey's rosy assumption that education was an inherently liberating process.

A later generation of adult education authors, most notably Stephen Brookfield, further complicated the picture by identifying how even teachers with good intentions—using a curriculum based on social change!—could be oppressive. Brookfield analyzed the different ways teachers held power, whether they liked it or not, and how that challenged the practice of teaching democracy.

I agree with all of it and I struggle with it all. I concur with Dewey that education must be grounded in students' experience, and I struggle to make that actually happen in my classroom. I agree with Freire that teachers can oppress, and do my best to teach my students some ideas around community organizing while also teaching the job interview skills they signed up for. And finally, I agree with Brookfield that the specter of teacher power hovers invisibly over the adult education classroom like the ghost of grandpa in "The Family Circus." But unlike Brookfield, I think the power that teachers wield is good for maximizing student learning.

We classroom teachers often have a chip on our shoulders when it comes to theory. We dismiss it as a luxury enjoyed by academics. But staying ignorant of the theories that inform our practice won't make that influence go away. Better to analyze and

15

consciously engage these ideas to take what is useful and cut out the rest.

EVERYTHING IN EDUCATION IS CONTESTED
Especially the stuff that is obviously true.

A lot of things in adult education seem obvious, and all of them are contested. Academics have built entire careers criticizing the common sense of our profession.

Now that may just be an argument against academics. I know that when I started teaching I didn't have time for any theories at all, much less for people disputing theories I didn't even know about yet. But with a few seasons under my belt I am more interested than ever in what the critics have to say.

One of the most provocative questions in adult education is whether learning should consist of more than acquiring new skills—particularly job skills. Stephen Brookfield, discussed in the previous section, concludes that if you only teach students the skills they need to do their jobs better, you're not teaching; you're just providing job training. In fact, you may inadvertently help keep students in the role society has set out for them, rather than helping them choose their own role (Brookfield, 2013, 86).

Feminist scholar Michael Collins goes one step further in critiquing, more or less, the Western take on adult education. He sees the focus on efficiency and serving businesses' training needs as working against the creation of a free society. Or, as paraphrased by Merriam et al., "adult educators are too concerned with how to plan programs or arrange a classroom at the expense of considering why some adults do not have access to education" (2007, 254).

The entire discipline of critical theory in education is dedicated to understanding education as a way to liberate people. This includes explicitly teaching students how to practice democracy and overcome the alienation in their lives (Merriam et al., 2007, 258).

Like many teachers, I pride myself on being able to teach concrete skills. It's important for that metric of success to be interrogated. In regards to education's purpose, I return to John Dewey: education should make more things matter. Education helps students make sense of their world and be able to choose their role in it. If your curriculum leads students down a steadily narrower path of specific job skills that help employers make more money from their labor, then you are training, not educating.

I do believe we need much more democratic decision making in our lives. To take just one example, as an activist I have gone to protests organized by the residents of the working-class black town of Richmond, California, to shut down the Chevron oil refinery there. In addition to contributing to the high rate of asthma in local children, the refinery caught fire in 2012, forcing a shelter-in-place for residents and sending dozens to the emergency room. And that was after an explosion at that same oil refinery in 1999!

With that said, as a teacher, I'd be hesitant to turn an ESL class in Richmond into a seminar about how horrible Chevron is. I would certainly write some stories for students about the company's role in the community. But to focus too much on Chevron, at the expense of English, is a loss to students who may not have the power to tell the teacher they're not getting what they need out of their ESL class.

I'm actually less likely to try to teach democracy because of my experience as an activist. I've developed my own practice of democracy through years of living collectively, through protests in the street, and through countless, countless meetings. Although I agree with the critical theorists about the importance of creating a democratic society, I respect democracy too much to make it the focus of my English classes.

(To their credit, critical theorists admit that their ideas do not easily translate into classroom practice. You can skip to Chapter 10 to see my big-picture ideas on how to make education truly more democratic.)

Note: *The fantastic education professor Jeff Andrade taught me how some teachers pride themselves so much on their belief in critical education theory that they never spend time actually learning how to teach. These teachers' radical politics actually diminish their teaching. Andrade's focus was on impoverished black and brown youth in the city, but I think his point applies to adult education as well.*

Note: *I focused on democracy and teaching because the topic is so juicy to me. Everything else in education is contested, too. There are theorists who criticize whether the teacher should be a distant facilitator or a caregiver, whether education should focus on individual students or on whole communities, and even whether we need a separate class of people trained to be teachers (!) (Merriam et al., 2007, 235–238).*

THE TEACHER DEVELOPMENT CYCLE

Behold my theory of teacher development!

The definition of a model is a simplified explanation of a complex process. With that in mind, Figure 1.2 is my model of teacher development. Based on the Kolb Learning Cycle, this model recognizes the importance of reflecting on personal experience to developing expertise.

It's through this cycle that teachers learn. Let me give you a typical example: you create your first lesson plan, struggle to teach it, and, upon reflection, realize your objectives were way too ambitious, which makes your plans for the following class more realistic, and so on.

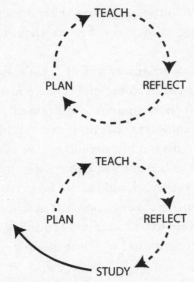

Figure 1.2 The praxis wheel
Source: Adapted from Kahn-Russell, 2012, 162–163.

There is no substitute for this deliberate process of planning, teaching, and reflecting. What this book offers you is a jump start. Through each section of this book, I'll show you how to improve your planning, your teaching, and your reflection.

TEACHING WILL MAKE YOU FEEL LIKE AN IDIOT

Or: A productive and inspiring way to approach your errors.

After eight years of teaching in the community, I briefly taught at a private ESL school for the first time. I thought I was doing a pretty good job. Then, after my second class ended, the academic director pulled me aside. One of my students had left the room, almost in tears, when I had criticized her for not doing her homework. I hadn't even noticed. (It turns out that students who pay a bunch of money to fly to the United States to study English have different customer service expectations than immigrants taking classes for free at their local community college.)

I felt like an idiot. And truthfully, that wasn't so bad. Every teacher feels like an idiot sometimes. The important thing is how you approach your shortcomings—with honest curiosity, without judgment. This is important because good teaching involves constant encounters with our shortcomings. We fail a lot, especially at first. [1]A good teacher always reflects on why students aren't learning as much as they should be, and how to improve our planning and execution. (In the situation just described, I realized that even though it's okay to be a hard-ass about homework, if I don't notice how my students feel, I'm not doing a good enough job paying attention.)

[1]Buddhists call the practice of always being open to learning new things "beginner's mind," and deliberately cultivate it as part

of their spiritual practice. People have been making this lemonade for a long time.

Note: *Teaching Will Make You Feel Like an Idiot was the original title of this book.*

TEACHING IS A TOUGH CAREER THAT KEEPS GETTING WORSE

Today's bad times are tomorrow's good old days.

Teaching adults used to be a great career. Back in the day—say, up through the 1990s—it was reasonable to think you could pay your dues for a few years at an institution, teaching those evening and weekend classes no one else wanted, and eventually get tenure and a sweet job for life.

Those days have gone the way of the mixtape. The education industry is transitioning to a mass production model where de-skilled instructors teach more students for less money with no job security or benefits. There's a generation of older teachers ahead of us holding the best jobs—which would be infuriating, except that they can't afford to retire, and even if they did, there's no guarantee their tenured positions won't be replaced by two part-time ones, neither of which would go to you.

Current trends in the profession—less full-time work, more privatization, huge online classes, and a glut of teachers—don't bode well for us. There's increasing stratification between the large majority of mediocre teachers willing to work crap hours for little money who will burn out in a couple of years and really

21

excellent teachers who get their pick of interesting assignments for life.

Which path will you pursue?

YOU WANT TO BE A GREAT TEACHER

It's as important for you as it is for your students.

Being a great teacher—one who maximizes student learning in the classroom, grows as a professional, and contributes to his or her field—is its own reward.

Great teachers have more fun. They're relaxed in the classroom because they've prepared the day's lesson, know (generally) what to expect, can manage their students' class experience, and look forward to taking advantage of any surprises that come their way.

Great teachers get more out of their teaching experience. They notice what students say (and don't), which informs their understanding of how students learn. Great teachers take what they come across in their everyday life—current events, popular culture, literature, and lived experience—and apply it to their teaching. That's why great teachers never get stale.

Great teachers walk the long path of becoming expert in their field. They follow the latest research and understand their field from all different perspectives, because they have to be able to explain it to students who come from all different perspectives.

Great teachers are respected by their peers. They're not just the king or queen of their classroom—that's easy. Great teachers post, publish, present, and otherwise contribute to their field. This impresses their bosses, too.

Finally, great teachers enjoy professional success. They often work for a variety of employers, challenging themselves by working in different settings with different student populations.

The irony is that it can be just as much work to be a bad teacher as a great one. Lesson planning at the last minute, panicking in front of your class, toiling in wretched institutions, living in constant fear of losing the job you hate anyway . . .

You should aspire to be a great teacher or quit now. It's too much work, for not enough money, to be mediocre.

NOTES

1. I learned about the discomfort zone from the social justice trainer George Lakey of Training for Change. See the bibliography for more on his fantastic book, *Facilitating Group Learning*.
2. David L. Chambers, Richard O. Lempert, and Terry K. Adams, "Doing Well and Doing Good: The Careers of Minority and White Graduates of the University of Michigan Law School," *University of Michigan Law School Law Quadrangle Notes*, Summer 1999: 60–71.
3. Samson, G., Grave, M., Weinstein, T., and Walberg, H., "Academic and occupational performance: A quantitative analysis," *American Educational Research Journal* 21, no. 2 (1984).
4. This quotation comes from a translation of Antoine de Saint-Exupery's *Citadel*. In the original: "Créer le navire ce n'est point tisser les toiles, forger les clous, lire les astres, mais bien donner le goût de la mer qui est un, et à la lumière duquel il n'est plus rien qui soit contradictoire mais communauté dans l'amour." Saint-Exupéry, A., and Lamblin, S. *Citadelle* (Paris: Gallimard, 1972).

KEY REQUEST FORM

TO: Laney College Key Controller, Business Office T-850

FROM: _____
        LAST NAME   FIRST NAME

DEPARTMENT: _____

ROOM   KEY#

[ ]   [ ]   DATE: _____

[ ]   [ ]   KEY CONTROLLER: _____

[ ]   [ ]

_____   KEY GUIDELINES AND
ADMINISTRATOR APPROVAL   REQUESTER SIGNATURE
                                      (OVER)
_____
BUSINESS OFFICER

CHAPTER 2

How to Get Started Teaching

READ YOUR TEACHING CONTRACT

Never sign anything you haven't read.

A contract is a legally enforceable promise. Every school you teach at will make you sign one. Reading it will make sure you know your obligations to your school and vice versa.

No matter what's in your contract, your school cannot violate state and federal labor law. Nevertheless, even big-name schools have failed to provide employees with benefits to which they were entitled, to name just one labor law violation. If you think something shady is going on where you teach, talk to a labor lawyer. Most will give you a free consultation.

Contract Checklist

Here are some specific points to look for in your contract:

- Wages for teaching time
- Wages for nonteaching time, if any: class prep, curriculum development, and so on
- How you will be evaluated
- How you can qualify for a raise or benefits
- Sick days, vacation days, and holidays (paid or unpaid)
- How you could be fired

YOU WORK FOR THE SCHOOL

Don't go rogue.

It's common for beginning teachers to think their new school is horrible. Maybe the administration is too demanding. Maybe the school's teaching methodologies are outdated. There is the temptation to ignore their rules and do what you think is best. After all, one of the benefits of teaching is the autonomy you enjoy in the classroom.

I suggest that you remember who you work for and not go rogue. Some policies may make sense after all. For example, you may have to submit detailed lesson plans so that your school keeps its accreditation. Other policies may never make sense. Either way, begin by making a good-faith effort to match your school's demands. As you gain experience and build your reputation as a good teacher, strategically choose which rules to bend. This can be the difference between getting a raise and getting fired.

YOUR FIRST YEAR'S A WASH

Your second year's not so hot, either.

Doctors and architects get advanced degrees and apprentice for years before going into practice on their own. Generally, if you want to teach adults, you just fill out a W-2.

That's an exaggeration. Adult ed teachers generally have subject matter expertise and maybe even a degree in their field. But most of us start without any training in teaching—and any training we do get rarely focuses on classroom instruction. That's a shame, because teaching is difficult. As a result, your first year of teaching usually isn't very good.

The first-year wash is especially problematic if you're teaching disadvantaged students. Too many instructors get their chops practicing on working-class or poor adults before moving on to students at more privileged institutions. For example, a new teacher may begin by teaching English in a community ESL class, and then switch to working for a private English language school that caters to rich students from abroad.

Please don't do this if you can help it. (For the record, I've stuck with teaching working-class students in Oakland my whole career.) If teaching adults isn't for you, there's no shame in transitioning out. The sooner, the better, for you and your students both! But if you plan to stick around, give those struggling students some of your good years to make up for the bad ones.

HAVE A MISSION

Your mission is the story of you.

On the first day of class you tell students about yourself: where you're from, why you teach, and how you ended up teaching this particular course. Internally, you should always think about your career interests and goals. This combination of public profile plus personal ambition is your mission.

Having a mission helps put you in control of your work and your life. On an everyday basis, your mission informs what directions you grow in. In a crisis, when your interests are in sharp conflict, it'll help you decide what to do in a way that's true to who you are and not determined by circumstance.

Story: At the end of one semester, a writing student I had failed came to me in a panic. She told me that her plan to take the following course, earn her associate's degree, and transfer to a four-year college were jeopardized by her failing grade.

I felt terrible for her. But after checking in with myself, I realized that my commitment to my institution (which was compromised by teachers regularly promoting unprepared students—probably how she ended up in my class in the first place) was such that I couldn't justify changing her grade. My mission kept me from doing something in the moment that I would've regretted for the rest of my career.

Note: The Seven Habits of Highly Effective People *by Stephen Covey has a good section on the importance of a personal mission statement and how to write one.* Man's Search for Meaning *by Viktor Frankl is the remarkable book that informed much of Covey's work.*

YOU CAN'T BE FRIENDS WITH YOUR STUDENTS

"Don't stand so close to me."
—*The Police* (Sting, 1980)

I don't think you can be friends with your students. Friendship is a relationship between peers, and as long as you have power over your students you are not their peer. When you befriend students you also risk caring more about your relationship than pushing them into their discomfort zone.

You can love and respect your students and everything they bring to class. But you still shouldn't friend them on Facebook. (I have only friended one or two former students, and even then only after they promoted out of my school and I knew I'd never teach them again.)

To help avoid any confusion, ensure that any out-of-class meetings with individual students occur in a public place. If you don't have an office, reserve a study room in the library or just meet in a local coffee shop. Never ask to meet students at your home or theirs. (Bars are probably a bad idea, too.)

Finally, don't date your students. In a noncredit program, you may be teaching skills they need to get a better job. In credit classes, your grade influences whether they promote to the next level, receive scholarships, or attain the degree they're working toward. An awkward breakup—which you might not even recognize as such—can do serious damage to a student's life.

If you date a student, you should be fired. If you do it again, you should probably be banned from teaching for life.

29

UNDERSTAND THE BUREAUCRACY

Master it so that it doesn't master you.

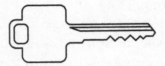

Once I got locked out of my classroom at my new community college job. My students and I stood outside in the rain for forty-five minutes until buildings and maintenance got us in—on my second day of class.

It was my most humbling episode in a career with no dearth of humiliation. It turned out that I needed a key form from the business office, signed by the department chair and the dean. No one had told me. Good times.

Your first task at a new school is to understand its bureaucracy. The sooner you do so, the sooner you can focus on teaching.

Know Your School Bureaucracy!

Here is a mostly comprehensive list of what you need to know to do your job. You can find the answers through a meeting with your department head or via an elaborate scavenger hunt.

- Academic policies (cheating, plagiarism, Americans with Disabilities Act (ADA) compliance, and so on)
- Academic deadlines (teachers dropping students, students dropping classes, posting grades, and so forth)
- Professional deadlines (submitting your syllabus to the department chair, and the like)
- For physical arts: Do students sign liability waivers? Does the school provide insurance?

- Room assignments
- Parking (Location? Need a permit?)
- Name and contact info for the department chair
- Whom to call if you're sick or running late
- Your office location and office hours (if any)
- Copy machine (Location? Need an access or department code?)
- Your school e-mail address and password
- Login info for any online grading or course management system (CMS)
- Is there Wi-Fi? Do you need a password?
- School ID (Do you need one to get into classrooms? To check out equipment?)
- Can you check out equipment? (laptops, projectors, and the like)
- Staff meeting times
- Professional development (in-house workshops or funds to attend conferences)
- Supply closet location
- Reimbursement policy
- Class break time policy
- Academic calendar (holidays, spring/summer/fall break, and so on)
- Final exam schedule
- How to apply for more or different assignments next semester

Note: *This list shows why it's hard to be a good teacher when you teach at more than one school. Bureaucracies are always different, even for two public schools in the same district. Mastering a second bureaucracy takes even more time away from your teaching.*

LOVE YOUR JOB

Love everything about it.

A key part of becoming a great teacher is to get the most out of every teaching assignment. This begins outside the classroom. Learn everything you can about your school. Get to know your colleagues, the official (and secret) history of the school, the different departments, and so on.

Always go beyond the minimum. Spend time observing other teachers, checking out the available teaching resources—especially if the school has a library—and going to all the unpaid meetings.

Finally, teach as much as you can: sub, volunteer, tutor, lead study sessions outside class hours. . . . Your learning curve is steepest at the beginning. If you teach a lot, you will improve quickly, and build a good reputation for yourself.

TEACH THE SAME THING

Repetition is a great teacher.

Nothing improves your ability to teach a class more than teaching it again right away. Your reflections can immediately be put into improving your lesson plans and teaching practice. Repeating a class builds your confidence, polishes your delivery, and deepens your understanding of the subject—including how students engage it.

Teaching the same class a second time or more is especially important at the beginning of your career, when your practice is shakiest. Having said that, don't be afraid to end classes at the end of the term if yours is a bad fit for you.

Story: I once taught the exact same class twice a day: same subject, materials, and student demographic. The morning class should have been better, because I would start it fresh as a daisy. But the afternoon class went better every time. From my experience in the morning class, I knew which activities would fly, which would crash, where students would get hung up, and where they might break through. I'd be hoarse at the beginning of the three-hour afternoon class and a little delirious by the end, but those students always learned more than the morning students. It's hard to overstate how much repetition improves your practice.

TEACH EVERYTHING

And do everything.

Later in your practice, variety becomes as important as repetition once was. You get tremendous insight teaching different levels and different students in different places. In my own career, I was surprised to learn that intermediate students needed almost as much repetition as beginning ones. I later discovered that there was a huge difference in ability between intermediate and advanced students—much greater than that between beginning and intermediate.

Variety extends beyond teaching. Try your hand at designing curriculum, leading workshops, proctoring exams, and more. Seize every opportunity you can. You never know where it will take you.

BE OPEN TO OBSERVATION

Only bad teachers don't like to get observed.

Most teachers are cagey about being observed. This is the legacy of bad management: at many schools, observations are done sporadically, evaluated arbitrarily, and then used as a pretense for firing teachers they didn't like. I can't tell you how many times I've asked to observe a veteran teacher and been rebuffed. Little old me!

I think this culture of aversion to observation blows darts. Peer observation is one of the best ways for new teachers to improve and for experienced teachers to keep improving. It allows you to instantly be exposed to new teaching techniques and even whole new perspectives on education. Observation is especially powerful when you observe another teacher who teaches the same class, or when you observe the teacher who had your students the semester before or will have them after you.

(An observation doesn't have to be time-consuming, either. You can observe for a half hour or even just a single activity.)

In exchange, be open to getting observed. This is wholly to your benefit. You foster a learning culture among teachers at your school and stay on top of your game. It's hard to get even a little lazy when a peer is watching you!

The only exception, in my opinion, is letting an administrator observe your class without notice. Administrators are often bound by regulations dictating how and when they can observe. If you start allowing them to observe you whenever they want, they'll pressure other teachers to be observed without following the correct process.

> *Hint:* Video recording your teaching lets you be an observer in your own class. Talk to an administrator to obtain both equipment and help analyzing the video. Many teachers

34

are immediately disappointed in their video performance —especially if you think you sound like Morgan Freeman and you actually sound like Marge Simpson. But once you get past that initial jolt you'll be amazed how much you can learn from watching yourself.

Observer Tasks

I always give my observers a specific task if they don't have one already. Here are some good tasks for classroom observation, in both academic and nonacademic settings.

- Promise Keepers: Does your class meet your objectives for it? How do you know?
- Learning with Purpose: Do students always know why they're doing what they're doing?
- Watch a Student: The observer surreptitiously watches a single student to see how they engage with the class.
- Listening to Instructions: Are they clear? Concise? Audible?
- Talk Time: How much does the teacher lecture? How much do students talk to each other?

LEARN TEACHER JARGON

It's the coin of the realm.

Being able to use education vocab is key to getting hired, publishing a book, negotiating with administrators, and generally succeeding in your career. The more you sound like a professional, the more you will be treated like one.

Knowing the jargon will also help you understand academic writing. It's especially good for searching for information. If you don't know the technical term for something, you won't be able to find out about it. (It's easier to search for "line of inquiry" than "starting a class with a really good question.")

Having said that, don't use jargon for its own sake. Like Rachel Carson once said about pesticides, the point is not to use as much as you can, but as little as you need to.

(See Appendix 1 for a glossary of teaching terms.)

BE ACTIVE IN YOUR UNION

Unions are the staunchest allies of teachers and students alike.

Most adult educators aren't in a union. That might not be bad if you're still finding out whether teaching is right for you. But a union is what makes teaching not just an enjoyable job but a sustainable career.

A union is a democratic organization of workers who collaborate for fair treatment and dignity at work. Unions negotiate a contract with management to ensure that all teachers get reasonable wages and working conditions, as opposed to each teacher individually negotiating their own salary and responsibilities. A union ensures that management plays by the rules, so that a lone teacher doesn't have to go up against the boss when the school violates the contract—or labor law. Without a union, workers are at the mercy of their employer's goodwill and good judgment.

Unions are crucial to education. What unions negotiate for— smaller classes, professional development, job security, and a living wage—are as important for students as they are for teachers. Unions also do crucial lobbying for education on a state and national level.

If you care about your students, your peers, your profession, and yourself, be active in your union. At a minimum, read your union newsletters to keep up with what's happening in your city and beyond. (Being active in your union is also a great way to network with other engaged professionals.)

If you stay at your job long enough there's a good chance you'll take a turn as a union officer. This can mean writing the newsletter, being shop steward, negotiating at the bargaining table, or even being president of your union local.

No matter how you participate, doing so is one of the best ways to engage in real democracy in America—at least compared to pressing a button in a voting booth once every two to four years.

What people think the learning curve is like.

What the learning curve actually looks like.

CHAPTER 3

How to Design Your Course

WHAT QUESTION WILL YOU START WITH?

If you don't start with a question, you'll end with one: "Who cares?"

In my opinion, the deepest learning comes from the search for answers to the questions we care about. Consider then how much time teachers spend giving students answers to questions they haven't even asked yet.

Begin your course—in planning and in the classroom—with one or two big questions that students will answer by the end of their time with you. These are often related to universal themes, such as success, power, and health—as well as failure, dependence, and death. Be able to articulate these questions in plain language your students can understand (Bain, 2004).

You can even start with a question that you don't know the answer to. For example, in an architecture class, identify a need in your city and design a project to address it. This will guarantee a high level of student engagement, because students won't be able to just regurgitate your own opinions back to you. However, this can be intimidating for new teachers, and tends to work best with higher-level students.

> **Note:** *In academia this is known as a "line of inquiry" or a "guiding question." These are core questions that students will not only engage throughout your course but also, ideally, throughout their lives.*

PLAN YOUR COURSE OBJECTIVES

These are the core concepts your students should walk away with.

It's been said that bad classes are based on activities, that mediocre classes are based on materials, and that good classes are based on objectives. Your course objectives are what students should be able to do by the end of your class. The extent to which they meet those objectives is the primary basis by which you evaluate your students' success at the end of the term—and your own.[1]

Objectives should be specific and measurable. "Students will know intermediate grammar" is not a good objective. A more detailed objective, such as "Students will be able to correctly use the simple past, past continuous, and present perfect in an academic essay," is much better.

Your objectives are the landmarks by which you guide the class. They determine which activities you choose, where you focus discussion, how you prioritize what to correct, and what you put on your final exam.

Bad Objectives

Following are some typical bad objectives:

- The Coverage Objective: "Students will go over the causes of the Civil War." This says how much stuff they will cover, not what they will learn.
- The Activity Objective: "Students will watch a documentary and discuss it with a partner." This says what they will do, not what they will learn.
- The Involvement Objective: "Students will enthusiastically sing an English-language song together." This says how they will do an activity, again, not what they'll learn.

Note: Industry commonly refers to "SMART goals," which are Specific, Measurable, Attainable, Relevant, and Timely. This is just a different way to describe good objectives.

FOCUS ON YOUR COURSE OBJECTIVES

Everything else is trivia.

After choosing your objectives, your first instinct is to choose a bunch of readings, activities, and assignments that somehow relate to the course—and to your various professional and personal interests.

Instead, think about how you can best help your students achieve the course objectives. This can be hard. One way to make it easier is to look at all those readings, activities, and assignments and make sure they relate to the big question(s) your course addresses.

The real hard part is the temptation to teach something simply because you find it interesting. There's an infinity of interesting (and important!) tangential things that won't fit into your class. If you follow every interesting tangent that presents itself, students may remember that trivia at the expense of your objectives.

> **Note:** *This doesn't mean you can never change your objectives! If you made a mistake in planning your course, it is your obligation to modify your objectives to best meet your students' needs.*

BREAK IT DOWN

> *"The only reason problems seem complicated is that you don't understand them well enough to make them simple."*
> —Myles Horton, Founder of the Highlander School
> (1998, 100)

One of our biggest teaching challenges is deconstructing our expert knowledge for students, such as how we make sense of a challenging reading, or how we make precise cuts on a chop saw. A good teacher must be able to break down a question, concept, or skill into its component parts.

For example, here's how I taught students to write a coming-of-age story for my Writing 4 class.

42

1. Students read a coming-of-age short story.
2. They identified its defining qualities: a young protagonist, a new challenge, a decision with lasting consequences, a transformation by the story's end.
3. Students brainstormed other coming-of-age stories.
4. They discussed their own personal coming-of-age stories.
5. They wrote down their personal story.
6. Finally, they checked their own story for the qualities they identified in that first story they analyzed.

Of course, I didn't actually teach it this way. I originally only broke it down into steps 1, 2, and 5 because I didn't know how hard it was going to be for my students to come up with their own coming-of-age stories. It was only when I was grading their papers—which weren't great—that I realized they needed structured activities to help them identify the turning points in their own lives.

Breaking concepts down is one of the hardest tasks for a beginning teacher. A great way to start is to look at how two different textbooks teach the same concept. Because publishers are all in competition with one another, their books almost always teach the same skills or ideas in different ways. Looking at different textbooks will give you insights into how to break it down for your students.

PLAN WITH THE END IN MIND

End with the plan in mind.

Veteran teachers plan their classes from the last day to the first. You work backwards to figure out how to get your students to your course objectives from what they already know—or at least, from what you think they know. (You haven't had your first-day assessment yet. See Chapter 4, "Start with a survey and an entry assessment.")

Planning backwards from specific course objectives makes planning individual lessons easier. Most teachers scramble to fill up each class period with random activities. It's far less work to choose activities that match your big picture than to scramble for purpose after going in different directions all term. In fact, you may have mostly unplanned days toward the middle of your course. You can plan these days when they come up—rather than two months ahead of time—when you have a better idea of where your students really are. (The education establishment fetishizes planning far more than teachers value it or students need it.)

One challenge is that your students will rarely get as far as you planned. The key is to prioritize what you want your students to get out of your class. Knowing what you absolutely want students to get out of your course will ensure that they arrive somewhere meaningful by the end of it.

I once taught a class on workplace communication twice, back to back. The first time I covered job interviews, deescalating angry customers, workplace harassment, professional e-mails, and teamwork, in that order. At the end of the course my students said they valued what they'd learned but wished they'd spent more time on job interviews.

The next time I taught the course I kept the syllabus the same, but I paid more attention to what students wanted to do. We ended up spending twice as much time on job interviews. We didn't have time for the e-mail and teamwork objectives, which was fine—I had put those at the end because I knew they were probably less important to students. As a result of these changes, these students could answer a wider variety of job interview questions, and answer them better, than the previous class could.

It may be enough to focus on a single overarching objective. One of the best classes I had in college was Constitutional Law, taught by the memorable (and memorably named) Ron Kahn. He ended the semester by saying he didn't expect us to remember every last case we had studied. Instead, we should have a general sense of the subject, so that when an authority said some BS about the constitution supporting their argument, we'd be able to think, "That doesn't sound right." Fifteen years later, that sticks with me.

A couple hours after that Con Law class I had my last Japanese Translation class. The professor ended with a series of random thoughts, including an admonition to use condoms (!). To be fair, fifteen years later, that's stuck with me, too. But was that the objective she had built the class around?

MAKE YOUR EXPECTATIONS CLEAR TO STUDENTS

I call this principle "No Surprises."

Once you've chosen your course objectives and mapped out how you'll meet them by the end of the term, you're ready to communicate this information to your students. I do so by the principle of "no surprises."

"No surprises" begins when you go over the syllabus on the first day (see the following section). Continue by clearly explaining each of your assignments and how you will grade them, from the first day's homework to the final project or exam. If your class is graded, tell students their midterm grade and their prospects for improving it (if necessary) before the end of the term. If the class is ungraded, let students know how they're doing otherwise. (For more on this topic, see Chapter 5, "Grade and evaluate students fairly.")

Sometimes you'll surprise students by doing something differently from what they're used to. For example, many students assume their tests will be multiple choice, and may be caught off

45

guard by essay questions. Sometimes the biggest surprises are things you don't think are surprising at all. (This is one reason it's so important to see the class from the student's perspective.)

You can follow "no surprises" and still choose to surprise your students sometimes—such as with a party or a pop quiz. Your surprise will be that much more effective because it won't be yet another random decision by the teacher.

SYLLABUSES ARE CRUCIAL

A syllabus is a contract and a blueprint.

A syllabus tells students exactly what they can expect from your course. It gives everything from the required reading to the date and time of the final exam. I suggest creating a syllabus-like document even if you don't teach in a classroom setting.

If we try to change our class without notice, a detailed syllabus is one of the few ways students can hold us accountable, so err on the side of being too specific and comprehensive. A syllabus can easily be four to five pages for a typical semester-long class.

You also write the syllabus for yourself! This is your blueprint for the next time you teach the class or for the next person who comes along to teach it. A halfway decent teacher should more or less be able to reverse-engineer the whole course from your syllabus. You are allowed to deviate from the syllabus, but do so for a reason. Tell students why and then update it ASAP.

Syllabus Checklist

Following are the items to include on your syllabus:

· Official course name and course number
· Class days, times, and room number/location

- Teacher name and contact info
- Course description
- What students will learn (course objectives)
- Course schedule and holidays
- What texts/materials students must buy (specify which edition)
- What students must bring to class: binders, textbooks, calculators, tools, and so on
- Classroom behavior expectations
- Classroom laptop/cell phone usage policy (Is Web browsing okay? Text messaging?)
- Absence and tardy policy (Can students come in late?)
- Late homework policy
- The school's honor code or cheating and plagiarism policy
- How you grade or evaluate assignments and tests
- Why you evaluate the way you do
- Your office hours, or how students can otherwise meet with you
- How quickly you respond to student queries (9–5, M–F by phone? 24/7 by e-mail?)
- Field trips, if any
- Class website, if any
- Outside resources: websites, books, and so forth
- The school's Americans with Disabilities Act (ADA) policy
- When, where, and in what format the final test will be administered

Hint: *At the bottom of my syllabuses I put a fill-in-the-blank for students to get the contact info for three other students. Because I always cover the whole syllabus the first day, every student has three different people to call for notes and homework if they miss class.*

Note: *The plural of "syllabus" really is "syllabuses," because Latin words of Greek origin that end in "-us" are pluralized "-uses." (Same goes for "octopus.") But if a colleague says "syllabi," you needn't correct them.*

TEXTBOOKS PROVIDE COURSE DESIGN TO TEACHERS

Students may buy the books, but it's teachers who choose them.

A good textbook does a lot of heavy lifting for teachers: choosing what material to present to students, sequencing it, providing practice exercises and even quizzes and tests. This is mighty appealing to a teacher faced with building a new class from scratch.

But textbooks are also an expensive straitjacket. A textbook is written to meet the needs of as many hypothetical students as possible—never for your particular students. If you slavishly follow the book you risk leaving some students behind who need additional practice, or meeting the author's objectives rather than your own.

Choose a good book. Then skip around and supplement it to meet the needs of your students and the objectives for your class. After all, if the only thing someone needed to teach your course was the textbook, couldn't any schmuck off the street do your job?

How to Choose a Textbook

Here's how to evaluate different textbooks to find the best one for your class.

- Table of contents: Does the book start where your students are starting and take them where they need to go? Do concepts progress in a logical way?
- Questions/problems for each section: Are they meaningful? How's the mix of quick and in-depth questions?
- Price: How much of the book will you use? Is it a good value? Will students have to buy a workbook or any other supplements, too?
- Digital supplements: Does the CD-ROM have additional activities and material? Is the online content just a partial copy of the book?
- Teacher's manual (if any): Does it provide alternatives if the student book activities don't work? Are the model answers clear? Is it easy to use as an in-class reference? Does it come with any additional material you need (audio CDs, and so on) or do you have to buy them separately?
- Teacher opinion: Do other instructors like this book? How does it compare to its competitors?
- Student opinion: What do they think of it?

USE TECHNOLOGY SPARINGLY

"If you think technology will solve your teaching problems, you don't understand the technology and you don't understand the problems."
—Paraphrased from Bruce Schneier, Security Technologist

Educational technology comes in many formats: Smart Boards, blogs, online surveys, and so on. These technologies are rarely the best way to accomplish any given instructional task. Instead, teachers often use them because they want to try them out.

Educational publishers are also pushing technology. They usually try to make a quick buck from poorly conceived digital content, such as online textbooks to which students lose access after a year, rather than pesky paper textbooks that students can resell at the end of the semester.

Technology should only be used when it's the best tool for the job. The best application of classroom technology I've seen is short video clips projected onto a big screen. Video can provide students with authentic material to observe, analyze, and/or criticize. Just have it on a CD or flash drive so you're not dependent on an Internet connection for the lesson to work—and so students don't have to wait in radio silence for the video to buffer. (Note that technology eats up precious class time, even when it works, and especially when it doesn't.)

Technology is like textbooks. The more you rely on technology to teach your course, the more replaceable you become. Instead of leaning on software "solutions," focus on giving students a learning experience that technology could never replace.

Tips for Evaluating Educational Software

Use this checklist to determine whether a piece of educational technology is worth your students' time.

- Will students access it enough to make it worthwhile?
- Is it Web-based, in which case students can use it from the library or computer lab? Or . . .
- Does software need to be installed, which makes it hard for students who share a computer with their family, or who don't have access to one at home?
- What's the login process? Do students need to create an account for it? If so, do they need an e-mail address? (Not all students use e-mail.)

50

- Must students answer questions the exact way the software expects? (Nothing is more frustrating for students than getting a correct answer marked wrong.)
- How easy is it for you to track students' progress?
- Are other teachers using this software? Will your students ever use it again?
- How is the tech support for students? For teachers?

PROGRESS IS UNEVEN; TAKE ADVANTAGE OF THIS

We often imagine progress as a steady upward path; it's actually all plateaus and ski jumps.

Students don't make constant, incremental progress, class by class, until they become experts in their field of study. Instead, students will plateau, even appear to get a bit worse, before making a breakthrough. (See Figure 3.1.)

Teachers must create an environment that cultivates breakthroughs. The most familiar example is the final exam. A big test lets you take advantage of the intense studying students do around midterms and finals. This is when they integrate what they've been learning and break through to a higher level of understanding.

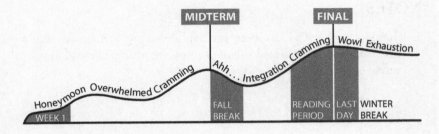

Figure 3.1 The learning curve for a typical college course

By the same token, respect breaks and vacations. Allow students to rest instead of making them work even more when they're least likely to get anything out of it.

If you teach an ongoing class, rather than a semester-based one, schedule culminating activities throughout the year, such as a live performance for the community, or an online publication. Without something bigger to work toward students are unlikely to make breakthroughs.

These tools can work for a traditional class as well. Veteran teacher Ron Berger says that in his class, "Every final draft . . . is done for an outside audience" (2003, 99). And he teaches elementary school! (See Chapter 5 for more on assessments.)

> **Note:** *Generally speaking, it's easiest for learners to progress from total novice to beginner, hardest to go from intermediate to advanced. Explain this to students who don't understand why they progressed so quickly before but now seem to take forever to improve. (And for an in-depth look at the learning curve, see the book* Mastery *by George Burr Leonard.)*

NOTES

1. Thanks to *The Skillful Teacher* by Jon Saphier and Robert Gower, along with *Teach Like a Champion* by Doug Lemov, for insight into "Plan your course objectives."

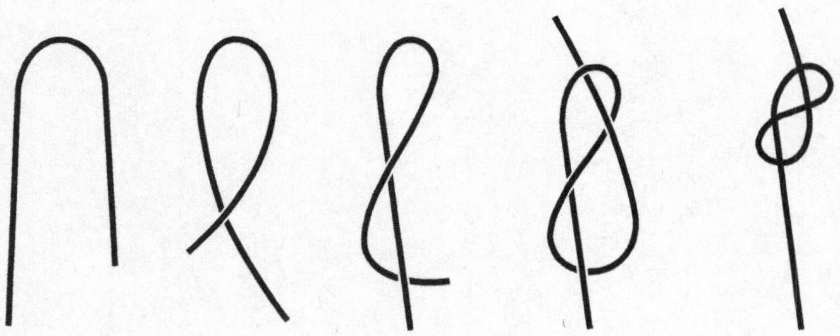

CHAPTER 4

How to Lesson Plan

THE FIRST DAY OF CLASS IS THE MOST IMPORTANT

Establish yourself as teacher and sell the class.

The first day is when most students decide whether to keep or drop a class. Perversely, it's also the day Murphy's Law comes out in full force. Being prepared for the first day will go a long way toward making your class successful.

I recommend dressing and acting more formally on the first day of class. This helps establish you as the teacher, especially if you don't match students' preconceived notions: you're young, small, the "wrong" gender for the subject, and so forth. As the term progresses it's easy to go from more formal to less formal; it's difficult to go the other way around.

Besides taking roll and going over your syllabus, there are a few things you should always do on the first day. First, give students a chance to meet each other. Without time to find out who their peers are and how they fit in, they'll be too distracted to learn anything (Lakey, 2010, 13). This is usually accomplished with an icebreaker, a structured activity where students learn about one another.

Second, make it clear that while you're on your students' side, their learning is their responsibility. Discuss how they can practice and study effectively for your class. (I lead an activity where students brainstorm how they maximize—and minimize—their learning.)

Third, especially for more novice learners (adults in a GED class, first-time yoga students) or for classes students traditionally have anxiety about (math, science, public speaking), acknowledge the fear or skepticism that students may have and make it clear that you're on their side.

Finally, sell the class. Introduce or elicit the questions students will explore in your course. Show them how exciting the topic is—probably through a short lecture or demonstration followed by a group work activity, so that students can engage the material and keep the energy level high. A lot of students shop for classes on the first day. Do your best to make sure they choose yours.

Pre–First Day Checklist

Do the following before your class begins to help ensure a smooth first day:

- Make a dry run of your commute to class
- Check the parking situation (Car or bike!)
- Find your room

- Look at the room setup (Fixed or moveable chairs? Big or small tables?)
- Check room resources (Whiteboard? Whiteboard markers?)
- Locate the nearest bathroom and water fountains (Do they work?)

First Day Checklist

Do the following in chronological order:

- Dress extra professional
- Show up thirty minutes early
- Set up the room
- Lay out your materials in the order you'll need them (markers, name tags, syllabuses . . .)
- Write your name and the course name and number on the board
- Welcome students as they come in
- Take roll and get students' names (note the pronunciation of their names, too)
- Have students do an icebreaker
- Introduce yourself
- Sell the class with an engaging lecture or activity
- Go over the entire syllabus (this may be done the second day of class)
- Answer any questions about the class
- Give the student survey and needs assessment (see the following section) and any other paperwork
- Assign any homework
- Answer any last questions
- Confirm the next class day, date, and time
- End class and stay after to answer any additional (or personal) questions

Note: *Handling the first day is especially challenging in open enrollment classes (such as yoga, karate, drop-in ESL classes)—where the most important day is each individual student's first day. Have a few set talking points and questions for new students, before and after class if possible. If nothing else, recognize them for coming to your class and see if they have any questions before they leave.*

START WITH A SURVEY AND AN ENTRY ASSESSMENT

The survey tells you who your students are; the entry assessment, where they're starting from.

Give students a survey to complete and return to you by the end of the first class. It should ask students about themselves and any factors that may affect their learning: legal name, the name they prefer to go by in class, contact info, educational history, past classroom or professional experience in the field, personal interests, scheduling conflicts, learning disabilities, physical limitations, and so forth.

The entry assessment is a series of questions or tasks based on your course objectives. It lets you see how close your students are to meeting those objectives already. Make it clear to your students that their performance on it won't be graded, collect assessments at the end of class, look at them when you get home, and don't give them back. These help you understand where the class is coming from and let you start adjusting the class for these specific students—not the hypothetical ones you or your textbook designed the course around.

For my writing class, every student writes a sample paragraph on the first day. This shows me where they are based on their grammar, paragraph structure, and use of academic language. It's helpful in no small part because I consistently overestimate my students' starting ability.

Finally, the entry assessment identifies students who are way below level—not just based on where I think they should be, but compared to their peers as well. I communicate privately with these students to let them know the class is probably too difficult for them, and recommend an alternative class better suited for them. If that doesn't convince such students to change classes, you can return students' first graded assignment before the add/drop deadline, to give them a reality check and a graceful exit opportunity (Davis, 2009, 414).

> **Note:** *If you test the same things with your entry assessment as you do with your final, it's also a benchmark test.*

GIVE 'EM A HOOK

Get students' attention and make them care.

When starting a new lesson, pique students' interest with a hook: a surprising fact or challenging question to draw them in.

A hook can be as simple as a famous quotation on the board for students to see as they come in, or a question about current events you ask at the beginning of class. A good hook will pique students' interest and encourage learning.

This is one more reason to know students' career and personal goals. You'll be able to create hooks not just for the entire

59

class but also for individual students—particularly those reluctant (or resistant) to engage your lesson.

Story: Last year I had to pitch my class on Workplace Communication to incoming students at my community college. I used the example of Air France Flight 447, because submarines had just retrieved its black box from the bottom of the Atlantic Ocean. When it first went down there was plenty of speculation. Were there faulty electronics on board the new Airbus 330? Was the crash due to the bad weather it was flying through?

The black box told the story. The bad weather triggered a failure of the plane's autopilot. No big deal; that's why we have two human pilots in the cockpit. However, due to erratic readings from sensors damaged by the weather, the pilot and copilot ended up giving contradictory commands to the plane. The plane crashed because one of the pilots was pulling up on his control yoke while the other was pushing down. Due to a lack of workplace communication, 228 people were killed.

That story was my hook for the class. It was probably my best work. (For more, see "Tell stories" below.)

TEACH THE DISCOMFORT ZONE

Teach it on the first day and refer to it throughout your class.

I will now give you my favorite lesson. This is how I teach the discomfort zone from Chapter 1.

On the first day of class my students always do an icebreaker activity where they introduce themselves to a partner and discuss a life experience that taught them something. (They will naturally choose something significant.) Then each student introduces his or her partner and the partner's learning experience to the whole class.

Most of the learning experiences students share will involve discomfort: a divorce, realizing their kids could run circles around them, a life-threatening motorcycle accident, and so on. After everyone finishes, I draw a modified version of the discomfort zone diagram on the board (see Figure 4.1) and talk about how, as we just saw, the most powerful learning happens when we are uncomfortable.

I summarize the ideas behind the discomfort zone and talk about how my job is to push them into their discomfort zone as much as possible. This basically becomes one of the ground rules for the class. You'll see that I don't include the alarm zone in my diagram or explanation because they'll use that as an excuse for not doing something that merely discomforts them.

I don't get much push back on the discomfort zone, perhaps because it's so abstract at this early stage. But for the rest of the term, when students tell me they don't want to try an activity I know is important, I'll remind them of the discomfort zone and they're more likely to try it.

Figure 4.1 Comfort zone/discomfort zone
Source: Training for Change.

PACE AND MOTIVATE WITHIN EACH LESSON PLAN

Start with an activity that builds energy, and end on a note that reinforces the day's lesson.

No matter how experienced a teacher you are, you should at least outline a lesson plan for each class. The newer you are to teaching, the more detailed your lesson plan will be.

Most lesson plans begin with an activity to get students motivated and to connect what they know to the day's objective. Partner or small-group work is one good way to get energy flowing, which is even more important with evening and early morning classes.

The basic rule for lesson planning: mix it up. You can extend one activity for a longer time or repeat a short activity a few times. For an hour-long class, students may do a group activity for twenty minutes or partner work with four different partners for five minutes each. They probably shouldn't do twenty minutes of group work followed by another twenty minutes with a different group, or do partner work with eight different partners for five minutes each.

End each class with three things. First, review the day's lesson. Second, connect it to the homework. Third, explain how the homework connects to what they'll learn in the next class. Connections that seem obvious to you may not be obvious to students. Explicitly relating the lesson to the homework and then to the next class will help students learn the material and motivate them to work on it.

If students have to turn something in before leaving (such as a quiz or reflection writing), have them turn it in to you personally; make eye contact with them and acknowledge their work before letting them leave. This gives a concrete ending to each student's class. It also motivates students to do well on their end-of-day task, rather than rush through it so that they can leave a bit sooner.

What to Include in Each Lesson

Here are a few things I check with each lesson plan. Do I . . .

· Start with a hook?
· Give students a reason to care about today's lesson?
· Connect today's learning with what they've learned before?
· Connect today's learning with the overall course objectives?
· Have visuals to illustrate what I'm teaching?
· Mix up activities?
· End by summarizing the lesson?

Note: In your lesson plan write down exactly how many minutes you plan to spend on each activity, and then note, during class, how many minutes you actually spent on each one. You won't stick to these times, but this practice will help you better predict how long activities take, which will help you lesson plan better in the future.

DEVELOP YOUR OWN MATERIALS
Start with Google and modify for your class.

Most lesson plans start with a Web search. Virtually anything you want to teach has been taught before, and there's the HTML to prove it. The only catch is that most teaching materials you find on the Internet are terrible. People post lesson plans that are just a string of unrelated activities. They post worksheets that contain factual errors. They post text riddled with obvious typos. (True example: "What was your favorite scene in the movie? Explain why?")

Having said that, there's enough good stuff out there that I usually start my lesson planning with Google, if only for inspiration. But I can count on one hand the number of times I've found materials online that meet my standards of content and presentation. Good teachers modify and create materials all the time. Following are a few tips to help you make the best materials you can.

The Handsome Handout

Follow these steps to make your handouts uniform, useful, and beautiful.[1]

- Use a serif font (like Times New Roman) for better readability.
- Use a readable font size: 18- to 24-point for titles, 14- to 18-point for headings, 10- to 12-point for text.
- Use the same font or two (max) for all your handouts. (I use a sans serif font like Arial for captions.)
- Write instructions at the top of every handout. Do you want students to read it for homework, answer the questions, and return it to you next class, or keep it as a reference?
- If students will fill it out and return it to you, put "Name: " at the top.
- Make titles and headings short and descriptive.
- Have ample margins, ideally one inch on each side, for readability and note taking.
- Put one line of blank space between paragraphs.
- Number everything for easy reference in class. ("Let's go to section II, question 1.")

- Number sections with Roman numerals; number questions with Arabic numerals.
- Include a few diagrams or pictures, as necessary.
- Label all diagrams and pictures, even if it seems obvious how they relate to the text.
- Cite your sources in your materials the same way you expect students to.
- Number your pages if there are three or more.
- Put your name and the class name in the footer, so students know it's for your class.
- Save your handouts in DOC and PDF format.

Hint: The most important quality in anything you create is brevity. The shorter it is, the more likely students will read it, the better they'll remember it, and the more useful it will be. Making it shorter will make it clearer, too. My handouts are typically one or two pages at most.

Hint: After spending hours on your materials you will inevitably find typos while using them in class. Do yourself a favor: mark any typos on your copy and fix 'em that night so your handouts will be perfect the next time you use them. Your future self will thank your present self for doing so.

SHARE YOUR MATERIALS FREELY

It's for the greater good and no one will pay you anyway.

Put your materials online and make them available in PDF and DOC formats. DOC is great for editing, whereas PDF lets people see what your handout is supposed to look like in case their computers misformat the DOC file.

This is good practice because you'll put more work into something your peers will see. In my opinion, sharing materials is also your professional obligation. It provides inspiration to others teaching the same classes, perhaps even giving them something they can use right away—thus saving them valuable hours of their life, hours you've already given up and will never get back. This goes double if your materials were inspired by something you found for free online.

Some teachers think they'll sell their awesome materials to other teachers for beaucoup bucks. But your potential customers will probably just look up a free (and crappy) version of whatever you wrote and use that instead. Indeed, if you hide your materials behind a paywall, how can other teachers even know if it's any good?

Develop a range of polished material to show off to potential employers. Putting my ESL stories online has led to several jobs creating material that in no way resembled my original work. I've also gotten kind e-mails from teachers around the world who have successfully used these stories in their classrooms. It's gratifying.

Finally, some people worry that if they give away all their ideas, they'll run out. Just the opposite is true. Giving away your ideas will force you to stay fresh. You won't be able to get away with doing the exact same thing over and over again. From my experience, the more I give away, the more mental space I have for new ideas. As the famous adman Paul Arden once said, "Give away everything you know, and more will come back to you" (2003, p. 30).

Story: I've written about 100 social justice stories and put them on my professional website. I was worried their . . . candid descriptions of American history would turn off potential employers. Instead, they've landed me several jobs, even if one of my employers told me, "I loved your ESL stories. You know you won't get to write anything like that here, right?"

DON'T GET TOO INVESTED IN WHAT YOU DESIGN.

> *"The things you own end up owning you."*
> —Tyler Durden, Pugilist, in *Fight Club* (1999)

One hazard of creating your own materials is that you can get locked into a way of teaching that doesn't meet your students' needs. You must candidly assess, early and often, if you're on the right track, and be ready to totally change your approach as needed.

Story: I once taught vocational English to Spanish- and Chinese-speaking apprentice carpenters. To help them learn carpentry vocabulary, I spent hours drawing and labeling shop tools for my handouts. (See Figure 4.2.)

The students were good at learning physical skills but didn't excel at reading my diagrams. Rather than switch things up, I made more diagrams, each more painstakingly detailed than the last. I had spent so many hours on them I wasn't able to acknowledge that this approach wasn't working for these particular students. So I made even more diagrams.

It would have been more effective (and a lot easier!) to change to a dialogue-oriented class. But I only figured that out months later. My students got more out of those two weeks of dialogue-based lessons than from all my handouts put together. And then the course was over.

67

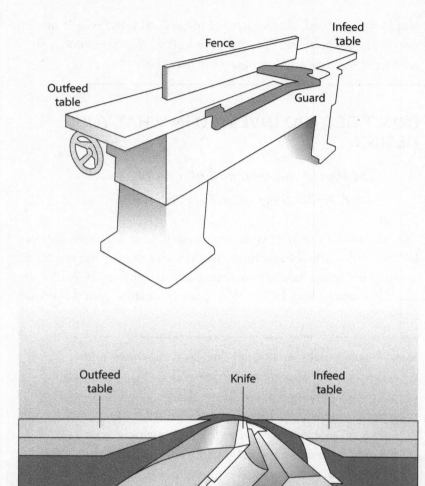

Figure 4.2 A jointer (with a "t") is used to make boards perfectly flat

"But lo! men have become the tools of their tools."
—Henry David Thoreau, Philosopher (1854/2013, 26)

TELL STORIES

Stories can pique interest and deepen understanding.

A story is a classic hook. Parables, or stories with an embedded question and no apparent answer, are especially good conversation starters. Why couldn't Moses enter the Promised Land? What did Bill Murray say to Scarlett Johansson at the end of *Lost in Translation*?

Like a good visual, stories can also illustrate what you teach. Newspapers do this all the time, pairing an article about the latest unemployment numbers with a gut-wrenching account of one family's experience with job loss and homelessness. Take advantage of that technique by telling stories to illustrate things that are important but abstract, such as statistics or safety rules.

Whether you're telling stories to get students' attention or to teach a lesson, maximize their impact by making them short, directly relevant to what you're teaching, and not all about you. (The exception is stories about mistakes the teacher made. Students always remember those.)

Whatever you do, don't tell all your stories. Just have them ready as one more way to explain things. If students get a concept without having to hear the story you prepared for it, that's a win for everybody. If you tell the story anyway, now you're wasting students' time to be the center of attention.

Sometimes humble stories work best. I recently got a climbing lesson from the people who train activists how to climb up tall buildings with big banners. One of the trainers used this story—the same one she used when teaching knots to fifth graders—to teach me the figure eight knot: You see a ghost, and it scares you so you run behind a tree, but then you think, "It's just a ghost," so you come back around and punch it in the face. (See Figure 4.3.) Ta da! Now I'll never forget how to make a figure eight, one of most solid and commonly used knots in climbing.

Figure 4.3 See a ghost getting punched in the face?

READY, FIRE, AIM

Act on inspiration, but reflect on it, too.

We all have great new ideas: using role plays to teach listening skills, using games to teach teamwork, using music to teach boxing . . . but most of these new ideas fail. That's OK, because the few that succeed can make a real difference for our students, our teaching practice, and maybe even the whole field we're a part of. (For an inspiring example, see the story in Chapter 9, "Administrators are people, too.")

If you're really excited to try something new in your class, you should probably do it. Engage in a process of discovery where you cultivate your new idea and find out where it fits into your course and your teaching practice. The key is reflection: What worked? What didn't? For whom? How do I know? How can I improve it next time?

Don't be afraid to set aside new ideas that don't work out. Focus on improving the promising ones and then share them with the rest of us.

> *"[Must] the teacher be cocksure about every single thing she plans to do? Must her intentions always be solidly grounded? Of course not. Teaching is a risky business. Missteps and unfortunate decisions are bound to occur. The person who is afraid of facing those risks definitely shouldn't be a teacher."*
> —Philip Jackson, *What Is Education?* (2011, 28)

MULTILEVEL CLASSES ARE HARD . . .

. . . and every class is multilevel.

Students in every class have a range of ability. Structure the course to engage everyone, taking advantage of students' differences rather than ignoring them.

For an explicitly multilevel class, such as a martial arts or ESL class with beginning through advanced students, you can start by having students work with others of the same level, and then switch to working with students of other levels for awhile. You can even pair up advanced and beginning students for in-class tutoring.

Another method is to give students stories or case studies to read. Beginning students can read them on a more surface level

71

while more advanced students may analyze them more deeply. In a short story class, novice fiction readers might look at plot and dialogue, while more experienced readers can see how a story matches or defies the conventions of the genre.

> **Hint:** *Open-ended questions are one of the best tools for a multilevel class. Try a low-stakes, open-ended question. I lead a two-hour "Know Your Rights" workshop based on role plays where someone interacts with the police, makes a mistake, and gets arrested. Each role play is followed by the question, "What did you see?" Because everyone sees something, everyone participates. I've successfully facilitated this workshop for audiences ranging from high school drop-outs to practicing lawyers, sometimes in the same workshop. (See Chapter 6, "Good questions are short and clear.")*

MAKE YOUR STUDENTS WRITE

> *"We do not write in order to be understood; we write in order to understand."*
> —Cecil Day-Lewis, Poet (Stanford, 2007, 227)

Students should write in almost every course they take. On the most basic level, writing can compel students to break down concepts step-by-step. This writing shows teachers what parts of a concept students are struggling with. This is why math teachers flip out when students skip steps (don't show their work), even if they get the answer right.

Writing is also an amazing tool for reflection. Often, we don't really know what we know (or believe) until we write it down. We all have different and contradictory understandings of the world. Writing helps you commit to an understanding—or to acknowledge and articulate your uncertainties. If students learn this process of reflection, they'll have developed one of the most important skills of lifelong learning.

Finally, writing is a private channel of communication between student and teacher. It's a chance for you to hear opinions and concerns students may not wish to air before the entire class or tell you face-to-face. (It's also a good way to become aware of and defuse problems before they blow up.)

Having said all that, most student writing isn't great. Here are a few tips for helping you and your students get the most out of their writing.

Getting the Most from Student Writing

Consider the following before crafting—and grading—any writing assignments:

- Know exactly what you want from the writing: How they're engaging with the class? Proof of basic comprehension? A beautiful piece of polished prose?
- Decide if the writing is for process or product. If it's a process-based assignment, from which you just want to learn how your students understand something, don't emphasize spelling, punctuation, and grammar. That will only make students self-conscious while adding little to what either of you get out of it.
- Explicitly communicate your expectation to students, orally and in writing. When you are disappointed by many students' writing, your expectations were probably unclear. (If clearer communication doesn't help, your expectations are probably too high.)
- Give students a model of what you want their writing to look like. (This can be a model you've written or a previous student's writing.)

- For product-based writing, let students know that revision is central to the writing process, even for experts. It's not as if Jay-Z walks into the studio and records a whole album on the first take.
- Try to have at least one round of revision built into the process, if not before it gets to you, then after you have evaluated it once. (Note that students will never revise an assignment they've received a final grade on.)
- When you evaluate students' writing, do so strictly based on your explicit expectations—typically a rubric. (See Chapter 5, "Write rubrics.")
- Give specific feedback: say at least one thing you sincerely like and, if there are edits to be made, tell them specifically what needs to be changed. Relate your comments to what you've discussed in class to help students connect their writing to their learning.
- Make your written comments legible.
- If it's not a writing class and students meet your basic expectations, let it go. Writing doesn't need to be perfect to be of use—to you or to your students.

HOMEWORK IS CRUCIAL

Review it in every class to bridge the previous lesson to the next one.

Class time is for answering questions, deepening prior learning, introducing new material, and assessing. If students spend class time only getting new information their progress will be glacial. It's like with piano lessons: the learning mostly happens between lessons, not during them.

To promote at-home learning, assign homework that pushes students to gather information and practice new skills between classes. I've given unemployed students homework where they had to write their first résumé. We reviewed them together in class to find errors, and students took them home to correct the mistakes they found. If we tried to correct every error in everyone's résumé in class we'd never get it done, and students would never the master the skill of correcting their own writing.

Many teachers collect homework at the end of class, grade it in a cursory fashion and hand it back a week or two later. Then they wonder why students don't try harder on it. Their students recognize that the homework isn't meaningful to the class or important to the teacher.

Reviewing homework in class shows students how important it is. You may go over every single question, which is comprehensive but time-consuming; you can cover a few parts to check for understanding (sampling from easy, medium, and difficult questions); students may correct their homework together and ask you to settle any disagreements they had; or you can use homework review as a springboard for small-group discussion or the beginning of class warm-up.

Another good reason to review homework in class is that it makes an individual student's failure to do the homework public knowledge. Avoiding that embarrassment may be a stronger incentive than a homework grade students don't see until the end of the semester.

PREPARE A SUB PLAN

Then find a sub.

It's a cliché that creating a lesson plan for your substitute is more work than just teaching class yourself. Having said that, if you have to be absent, you need to give your sub a lesson plan. There are two ways to prepare one: ahead of time or right when you need it.

The advantage of preparing a sub plan ahead of time is that it'll be ready when you suddenly, unexpectedly need it. The downside is that your lesson plan will have to be generic, with a few blanks to fill in for the specific class you're missing. (For example, beginning the sub plan with students discussing whatever their homework was before having them read "pages ___ to ___" in the book and discussing it with a partner.)

The advantage of creating your sub plan right when you need it is that it can be crafted based on exactly what you're doing in class that week. The disadvantage is that it's a hassle to put one together when you're already sick or otherwise in crisis.

Even the best sub plan can't teach itself. In every school I've taught in, it was basically the teacher's job to find their own substitute. (That person had to be an approved sub, of course.) The reasons were many. The schools couldn't reliably find subs, or different subs had wildly different teaching styles, or some were only suited for specific classes while others were terrible at everything. In practice, the teacher had to contact the sub first and then tell the school they'd be absent and who their sub was going to be. (I avoid telling students when I'll be absent because they'll often skip class if I'm not there. Other teachers make a point of preparing students for a substitute.)

Finding a substitute can be as easy as talking to a peer who has taught your class before or asking colleagues who the good subs are. Either way, get the sub's e-mail and phone number and give him or her the following information.

What to Give Your Sub

Make sure you give these details to your substitute so that class can go smoothly in your absence.

76

- The logistics: Class time, date, room number, and the key to get in (if needed)
- Materials: Lesson plan and the correct number of handouts for the class
- Student info: How many to expect, if any have special needs, and so on
- What to do after class: Put students' papers in your school mailbox or desk drawer, and so forth

Story: I was once teaching a class during which I felt progressively more ill throughout the day. After much contemplation—and vomiting in the bathroom while students were doing a worksheet—I let the class out fifteen minutes early.

I'd never done this before and was worried students would think I was unprofessional. Instead, they looked relieved. I thought back on how distracted they'd been and realized they must have seen me getting sicker before their very eyes. If you become too sick to teach, call your administrator, give a heads-up to whoever is teaching next door, end class early, and go to bed. Students can't learn when they're worried about the teacher.

END EACH CLASS ON A STRONG NOTE

Students remember the end of class best.

Just like the end of the term, the end of each class is the best time to reinforce what students are supposed to take home. Whether by summarizing the lesson or quizzing students to check for and deepen understanding, make the end of each class matter.

If students spend the last few minutes packing up (or leaving early), call them on it. By saying—and showing—that the end of class is the most important part, you give a good reason for them to stay focused.

If you usually end class with administrative tasks like collecting homework, push that up a bit so that the end of class is open for a really strong close.

Note: Research shows that students who write summaries of classes (or readings, or lectures) do better in classes than students who don't (Davis, 2009, 310).

NOTE

1. Thanks to teacher friend Stacy Nelson for many of the tips from "The Handsome Handout" (her title).

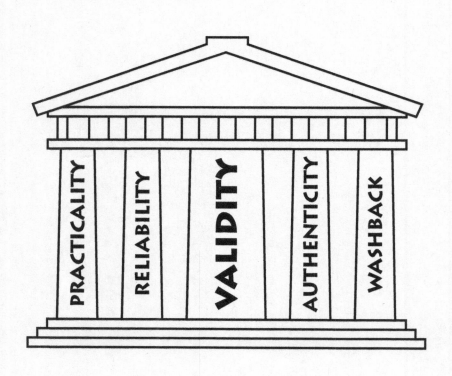

CHAPTER 5

Grading and Assessments

ASSESSMENTS ARE HARD, FRAUGHT, AND CRUCIAL

It's been said that if you can't measure it, you can't improve it.

There are two kinds of assessments. Formative assessments are surveys which let students evaluate the class format: lectures, activities, assignments, and so on (FORMative assessments, if you will). Summative assessments measure what students have learned. The classic summative assessment is a test, but verbally asking students questions in class is a summative assessment as well.

You design summative assessments around your course, and vice versa. You write them based on what you want students to be able to do by the end of the class. Conversely, what you teach on a day-to-day basis is informed by students' performance on your assessments.[1]

Summative assessments are ethically fraught. Do we test students on the skills they need to be a CEO? An assembly-line worker? An academic? And what kind of assessment should we use: a paper test that's easy to grade but doesn't reflect real-world demands, or a portfolio project that better reflects real-work tasks but takes multiple classes to explain and is a pain in the ass to grade?

An assessment is a two-way conversation. The teacher tells individual students how they're doing in the course. In return, the class collectively tells the instructor how well she is teaching. If a bunch of students make the same mistake, that tells you something. If a bunch of students make a bunch of different mistakes, that tells you something, too. Evaluate your students' assessments quickly, but don't return them before you've reflected on what they told you.

THE FIVE PRINCIPLES OF ASSESSMENT

These "five principles" aren't administrators in your school district.

Testing is an enormously complicated field. Fortunately, you can break down assessment theory into five basic principles.[2]

The Five Core Principles of Summative Assessment

Evaluate your assessments based on these principles:

1. *Practicality.* How quick and easy is it to create, administer, and grade the test? Practicality includes coming up with tests that don't take more time to complete than the class is long, or don't have so many different correct answers that they're impossible to grade.

2. *Reliability.* Can the test be graded objectively, or are the questions hopelessly subjective? Will two different teachers give the same student two different scores? Will the same teacher give two students at the same level different scores if they're tired, grumpy, or don't like one of the students? (See the upcoming section "Write rubrics" for help with reliability.)

3. *Validity.* Does the test actually measure the knowledge or skill it's supposed to? (More on validity to come.)

4. *Authenticity.* Does the test assess students' ability to perform in real-world situations, or are the test questions and situations contrived? We shouldn't give tests so inauthentic that they don't reflect real-world demands. But if a test's tasks are too authentic they'll probably require students to use many different skills at the same time, which makes it hard to figure out what exactly students don't know when they get something wrong.

5. *Washback.* Does the test make it possible for the teacher and student to improve student learning based on its results? A test that requires students to show every step of their process—like showing all their math work, or designing every piece of a carpentry project before assembling the project itself—provides more washback at the expense of authenticity. You, the teacher, get to see exactly where students went wrong, but students probably won't spell out every single step when doing these tasks out in the real world. And it feels unfair when a student builds the carpentry project correctly but gets marked down for not designing all the pieces ahead of time.

As you can see, the five principles exist in tension with one another. If you test just one skill, you make the assessment more valid but less authentic. Spending lots of time writing rubrics improves reliability but reduces practicality. And so on.

There's no such thing as a perfect test. But if you apply these five principles your assessments will already be better than most.

Note: Don't assume that assessments from textbooks, or your department, or your peers, necessarily meet these five principles!

VALIDITY IS THE MOST IMPORTANT PART OF A TEST

Test what you teach.

Of the five core principles of summative assessment, the one violated most often is validity. This is unfortunate, because validity is also the most important. After all, the main reason you give a test is to see if students have learned what you taught them.

I see this in ESL classes all the time. Let's say a teacher wants to test students' listening comprehension. The teacher has students listen to a short audio passage and write answers to questions written out on a paper test. Now take a moment to identify what's wrong here.

The problem is that the teacher is now testing students on their listening, reading, and writing skills. To be valid the teacher must make sure the reading and writing required to complete the task correctly is easy for students at this level, to ensure that any wrong answers are due to problems with comprehending the listening passage, not with reading the questions or writing the answers. (Better still, the answers should be multiple choice, to eliminate writing as a possible source of error. This comes at the expense of authenticity but is probably worth it.)

Most teachers quickly learn to make their tests practical. Rubrics make tests pretty reliable, too. Reflecting on tests and talking to students about their performance will help you achieve washback. I personally believe that teachers spend too much time worrying about authenticity and not enough on validity. Focus on validity to ensure you're testing what you're teaching.

GRADE AND EVALUATE STUDENTS FAIRLY

Fair as in reasonable, fair as in consistent.

Students want to know how much they've learned. However, it's difficult for students, especially novice learners, to evaluate their own progress. Students want and need a way to measure their learning. This is typically done with grades or other standard evaluations, like a certificate of completion, or a black belt.

Let's start with grading. Grading consists of two things: fairly evaluating each individual assignment ("75%," or "passing") and putting that assignment in context with the overall class objectives (deciding if it's worth 10 or 40 percent of the final grade).

I always make the final project or exam cumulative. Even if it's weighted so that most of the questions (and most of the points) are based on what we studied at the end of the course, which should be the meatiest content because you've spent weeks or months building up to it, I always include at least some questions on what we've studied from the beginning of the term. That way, if students take a while to learn earlier content they struggled with, they're rewarded for having finally gotten it. Otherwise, you're encouraging successful students to forget what they've learned and discouraging struggling students from even trying to master the stuff they didn't get the first time around.

I also make the final a large part of their grade so students work hard on it, even if they're going into it with a bad grade. If the final isn't worth much, you're encouraging struggling students to just give up by the end.

A fair evaluation scheme is still important for classes without grades. Will you give students a written evaluation? Verbal feedback in a one-to-one meeting? Self-reflection is also a legitimate form of evaluation. In addition to being a good skill to teach students, studies show that student self-evaluations closely match teacher evaluations when they aren't high-stakes.

A GRADE DOESN'T MEASURE HOW MUCH YOU LIKE YOUR STUDENTS

"F" stands for "Feedback."

You will inevitably have students you don't care for who get a better final grade than you think they deserve. And there will always, always be a student you love who doesn't pass the course. That's a sign of success. It means your grades aren't a measure of how much you like your students.

The more you separate grades from feelings, the better. This will keep you from penalizing students just because you don't like them—and you may dislike them for reasons that have nothing to do with their learning. For example, I had a classmate in college who would ask reactionary questions during class and then write thoughtful essays for his homework. His process was obnoxious but his learning was real. Students who annoy you shouldn't be punished for it.

By the same token, you shouldn't give students a better grade simply because you like them. It's a dangerous rabbit hole to go down. If your rubrics are fair, they'll get the grades they deserve. The more objective your grades, the less guilty you'll feel when you inevitably don't pass those students you love.

In fact, when you pass failing students, you're letting yourself off the hook. If students who work hard fail your class, the problem is likely your teaching. Instead of giving false charity—making yourself look generous while setting up your students for failure by sending them on to a class for which you have not prepared them—evaluate your teaching and see what went wrong. By promoting students who haven't earned it, you're passing yourself when you probably failed.

WRITE RUBRICS

Rubrics are key to quick and consistent grading.

Creating a rubric helps me break down what I'm teaching and how important the different parts of it are. The completed rubric clearly communicates my priorities and expectations to students. (See Table 5.1.)

Changing your rubric when it falls short will help you understand where students are coming from and what they need. For example, a category in your rubric may be too vague: "Correct punctuation (10 points)" then becomes "The first word of every sentence is capitalized (3 points)," "Two spaces after every period, question mark, or exclamation point (2 points)," and "Correct use of commas (5 points)." As students develop more skills, the rubrics you give them will become more detailed and demanding.

I have students evaluate their own papers with my rubric before they turn them in to me. This encourages students to look at their papers the same way I do. (The ability to read your own

Table 5.1: Sample Rubric for a PowerPoint Presentation

Spoke to the class confidently and naturally	0–10 points	points
Did not read the slides verbatim	0–5 points	points
Slides were titled and had between four and six points	0–5 points	points
Slides logically built up to a strong conclusion	0–15 points	points
Q&A: Repeated students' questions and answered them	0–15 points	points
	Total: ___ points	

One thing I liked:

One thing to improve:

writing from the perspective of the reader is one of the most important skills a writer can develop.) I will then fill out another copy of that same rubric and use it to grade their papers.

Rubrics are useful for ensuring that different instructors teaching the same class actually teach the same thing. You can also compare rubrics between two levels of the same class (Writing II and Writing III) to see how directly class skills build off each other.

"CLASS PARTICIPATION" GRADES ARE MOSTLY BS

But class participation is still important.

When you give students an assignment you should be able to tell them exactly how you will evaluate it. This is impossible with class participation. Is good class participation asking a bunch of different questions? Asking a few really good ones? Does a student who just gives the answers to their classmates during group work earn a better grade than one who struggles to keep up with peers? Imagine trying to create a rubric for class participation. It's too hard to meaningfully quantify, much less track, for every student, every class.

For all its nonspecificity, I do appreciate that a class participation grade recognizes that students are partially responsible for each other's learning. Asking questions and volunteering answers helps everyone learn more. That should be valued. I generally make class participation 10 percent of the final grade for that reason.

Keeping class participation a relatively small part of the final grade keeps the class transparent. Making it a huge part hides students' grades until the end of the term, when it's too late for them to do anything about it. Rather than a big class participation grade, it's better to have meaningful in-class activities that you grade objectively. And if students miss an activity due to an unexcused absence, they get a goose egg on it.

HOW TO WRITE A FORMATIVE ASSESSMENT

It's like a test with no wrong answers.

Most teachers do only one formative assessment, at the end of the semester, when it's too late for it to make any difference. As a result, what little students say about the teacher and class is bland and positive. These are known in the industry as "smile sheets."

Far better to do several formative assessments through the term. Do a short one a few weeks into the term. (To beginning ESL students I explain that it's like a test with no wrong answers.) When they see you adjust class based on their feedback, students will take their formative assessments seriously.

A good time for a more comprehensive formative assessment is midway through the course. Look at students' feedback—as well as their grades—during the spring or fall break, and consider changing the second half of the course accordingly.

Formative Assessment Questions

Following are some questions you can use on almost any formative assessment:

· What's the most important thing you've learned so far?
· What's been most difficult to learn?
· How difficult is the homework?
     (Least difficult) 1 2 3 4 5 6 7 8 9 10 (Most difficult)
· How interesting is the reading?
     (Least interesting) 1 2 3 4 5 6 7 8 9 10 (Most interesting)
· What activities have been most helpful so far? What activities have been least helpful?
· What activities would you like to do more of? What do you want to do less of?
· What's one way I can improve the class for you?
· What can you do to learn more in this class?
· Are you on track to meeting your learning goals for this class?

Story: So I'm teaching my very first class at the community college I always wanted to work for. The administration gives my students a formative assessment midway through the semester. I'm terrified. For various reasons, I had needed to completely change the course from what I had initially planned, and it continued to be a work in progress. I see that one of the questions is, "Does the teacher have a plan for what you will learn?" I wonder, "Does he?"

   My students were incredibly kind on the assessment. (The administrator who looked at them wrote "Nice!" on the summary page.) Truth is, about 95 percent of the student feedback I've gotten has been, perhaps, too kind. You will quickly learn not to fear negative feedback but to hanker for it.

Note: *You can also build quick formative assessments into everyday lesson plans. For example, I've finished workshops and classes by asking, "What's the most important thing you learned today?" This makes students reflect and make sense of what you've taught them. It also gives you valuable data on what students are getting out of your instruction.*

HOW TO WRITE A SUMMATIVE ASSESSMENT

The only thing worse than taking a test? Writing one.

Even a classic, boring, paper-based assessment is hard to write well. Here are some tips for creating a useful quiz or test.[3]

True/False Questions . . .

Are good for quickly testing recall of a large body of material. Here are some tips for writing triumphant true/false questions:

· Use short, declarative sentences.
· Avoid ambiguous words like "often" and "usually."
· Ask enough true/false questions to justify their use.
· Use variations when appropriate: Is a sample sentence fact or opinion (F/O)?

Multiple Choice Questions . . .

Are quick to grade like true/false questions but more difficult for students to answer, and for teachers to write. Here are some tips for writing marvelous multiple choice questions:

· Avoid ambiguous words like "often" and "usually."
· Have at least four possible answers to each question to minimize lucky guessing.
· Keep possible answers about the same length.
· The correct answer should clearly be the best one.

Short Answer Questions . . .

Show what students have successfully memorized. Here are some tips for writing sharp short answer questions:

· Tell students if their answer needs to be a complete sentence.
· Ask students to define vocabulary or identify key figures and concepts. (In other words, check if they've memorized the things from your class worth memorizing.)
· Don't make students analyze or do other high-order thinking. Check memorization only.

Essay Questions . . .

Show how students understand and engage the concepts in your class. They're also difficult to craft and, potentially, a pain in the butt to grade. Here are some tips for writing excellent essay questions:

· Tell students approximately how many paragraphs (or pages) their answers should be.

- Clearly state what you expect: A summary of knowledge, an application of it (such as solving a problem), or another skill.
- State whether students will be graded on grammar or punctuation.
- Offer several questions that students can choose from so they have more opportunities to demonstrate what they've learned.
- Make sure the questions match your stated course objectives.
- Use questions based closely on those used in classroom discussion or homework.

Overall Summative Assessment Design Tips

No matter which kinds of questions you put on your test, following the advice given here will make life better for both you and your students.

- Start writing it early enough to be able to give students a good idea of what will be on it.
- Write how many points each question is worth to help students prioritize what to answer.
- Put the most difficult question at the end of each section (for example, put the hardest multiple choice question last), so students won't fixate on it and not finish the section.
- Make the questions on the skills students learned at the end of the term worth the most points, because they should be the most difficult.
- Take the test yourself. Are the instructions clear? Is there enough space to write the answers?
- Time yourself. It'll take students two to three times longer to complete the test.
- Show your test, along with your model answers, to a colleague to see if it's fair.

- Make sure students are prepared for the types of questions (T/F, essay) on it.
- After students take the test and you've reviewed it together, correct any errors you find (clarifying instructions, fixing too-easy questions, and so on).
- Use the corrected assessment as a practice test the next time you teach the course.

HOW TO GIVE A TEST

My best practices for administering a test.

No one ever taught me how to give a test. Below are the best practices I've figured out for doing so. These rules are on the stricter side because I teach in an academic setting; feel free to alter them based on your context. (I try to apply these rules to quizzes, too, so there are no surprises on the day of the final exam.)

Before the Test

1. Ideally, space students so they're not sitting right next to, in front of, or behind each other.
2. Separate students who are good friends.
3. Have students clear their desks of everything not specifically permitted.
   - Visually check each desk before proceeding.
4. Pass out the test and go over it together, including the instructions for each section.
5. Answer any remaining student questions.
6. Explain that the use of anything with a screen is forbidden during the test.
   - Have students turn off their phones.

7. Be clear if students will be allowed to leave the room during the test.
    · If not, give them a final chance to get water or use the bathroom.
8. Tell students to personally hand you their tests before leaving.
9. Have everyone begin taking the test at the same time.

During the Test

· Stay in the room the entire time.
· Approach students who appear confused, frustrated, or make eye contact with you.
· Every ten minutes or so, ask if anyone has a question.
· Periodically walk around the class. Look for students who are:
    · Doing activities incorrectly (giving single-sentence answers to essay questions, and so on).
    · Falling way behind (or getting way ahead) of everyone else.
    · Totally stuck.
· Give warnings at ten minutes, five minutes, and two minutes remaining to finish.

When Students Finish

1. Have each student go to your desk and personally hand his or her test to you.
2. Before the student walks away, make sure every question on the test is answered.
    · If not, and there's time left, send the student back to sit down attempt the unfinished questions.
3. Make eye contact and thank students for their effort before letting them return to their seats or leave class.

BE CRITICAL WITH THE FACTS

You are a scientist, not a creationist.

You can collect data with each question you ask students, each activity, each quiz and test. What percentage of students understand various concepts? Who in particular is getting things right? What's their thought process when they're wrong?

Like a scientist, look hardest at the data you don't like. Don't be disappointed or frustrated—because it's not about you. Look hard at students' progress over the term, how they compare to other teachers' students, as well as to students you've taught in the past.

The earlier you start collecting facts, the earlier you can deal with unexpected results. If you wait, you can fall into a downward spiral where you don't like what you see, don't change anything because you're in denial, and then get even worse results later on—such as on the final exam. It's better for everyone if you change things early and immediately, based on where students really are, not just where you want them to be.

BE KIND TO YOURSELF

Don't make teaching harder than it already is.

One of the hardest things you'll ever do is teach a class for the first time. At the beginning of your career, make a strong request to your administration to teach the same class at least two consecutive times. If you feel yourself really struggling, this might be enough to quit over.

By the same token, be open to happy surprises. My evening ESL class, which students attended from 6 p.m. to 9 p.m. after working all day, was a pleasure to teach because the students were so motivated. On the other hand, my happily unemployed daytime students were less motivated, less successful, and way less fun to teach. (That Cuban guy with the Japanese radical labor history? Evening student. The class that abandoned me just because I taught poorly? Daytime students.)

Easy Versus Difficult Classes

Below are the factors that distinguish an easy-to-teach class from a difficult one. Can you guess which ones beginning instructors are more likely to be given?

Easy	Difficult
Optional course	Required course
Fewer students	More students
Meets 2 to 3 times a week	Meets once (or 5 times) a week
Experienced students	First-time students
Established class	Brand-new class
Free for students	Not free
Teacher gets a desk	No place to store stuff
No administrators on site	Administrators on site

STANDARDS ARE ASSESSMENTS FOR TEACHERS

How will you measure your success?

There are few standards in adult education; this is a blessing and a curse. Over your career, you may literally never be held accountable to any particular standard of student success in your class. You'll be evaluated instead on a more arbitrary basis, such as your popularity with students or how well you play ball with administrators. (There are no standards for administrators, either. Just saying.)

A clear, measurable standard is key to meaningful reflection and development. How will you measure your success?

Types of Standards

Following are some standards you can use to evaluate your success as a teacher:

· A standard based on your students last year
· A common standard with other teachers at your school
· A standard based on what students need to begin the next level
· A common standard with other teachers in your district
· A standard based on what employers in your region (or industry) want
· A standard based on how many students pass an outside certification or other exam
· A standard students choose at the beginning of the term

NOTES

1. *The Chicago Handbook for Teachers* has an excellent section on assessments. *What the Best College Teachers Do* also gives good insight into grading systems that maximize student learning.
2. For help with understanding the five principles of assessment design, thanks to Dr. Priya Abeywickrama, Dr. Doug Brown, and Dr. Eddy White.
3. For "How to write a summative assessment," thanks to *A Handbook for Adjunct/Part-Time Faculty and Teachers of Adults* by Donald Greive, EdD, and *The Art of Teaching Adults* by Peter Renner.

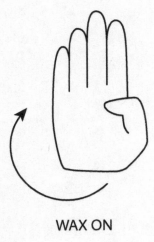

WAX ON

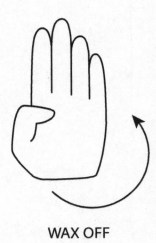

WAX OFF

CHAPTER 6

How to Run Your Class

START ON TIME

As they say in yoga, "Start on time to honor the practice, end on time to honor the student."

Adult students are often late to class. You may be tempted to delay class, just a bit, until more students arrive. Big mistake. When you start late, you punish students who come on time and soon everyone will come late.

Having said that, I am loathe to discipline students for being tardy. Adult students are typically late for good reason. They may have to work overtime, can't find parking, or need to take care of their family when someone gets sick. A better way to encourage promptness is to do something meaningful at the beginning of class that rewards those who come on time without unduly punishing latecomers.

In my ESL class, I asked on-time students what they did over the weekend to see which irregular verbs to review. ("I go to work this morning.") Other teachers did pronunciation exercises tailored to the needs of the few students present at the starting bell, because teaching pronunciation to many students who speak different languages is impractical.

You can't make every student come on time. Doing something meaningful at the start of class encourages students to come as early as they can.

START AND FINISH EACH CLASS THE SAME WAY

Rituals are part of every community.

An opening ritual is a powerful way to promote learning. They help students leave their problems outside and focus on class. At my dojo we bow before getting on or off the training mat. It only takes a few seconds, but it's a powerful reminder to focus on our training, which is important for our safety as well as our practice.

Rituals also help establish community. It's the difference between a unified class that learns together and a bunch of strangers who all show up to get what they want, and then get out as soon as possible. Beginning- and end-of-class rituals minimize students trickling in and out.

> **Example:** *I begin every class by looking at each of the students as they come in and saying, "Welcome." I end every class by asking all my students, "Good class today?" ("Yes!") "See you tomorrow?" ("Yes!") The enthusiasm—or lack thereof—in their answer helps me know how good a job I did.*

Note: *Popular educator Levana Saxon starts and ends class with a check-in and check-out. For example, "What's one word that describes your mood?" or "What's your personal weather report today?" (Students can describe themselves as "Sunny," "Dark and stormy," and so forth.)*

BUILD TRUST TO MAXIMIZE LEARNING

A student's trust in the teacher and other students makes it possible to take risks.

Trust makes it possible for students to get into their discomfort zone, without falling into their alarm zone and shutting down. With trust, students ask questions, give answers, and attempt things they couldn't do before. This is where learning lives.[1]

Creating an environment where students trust you and each other is known in the literature as "building the container." The stronger the container, the bigger the risks you can take and the more everyone will learn (Lakey, 2010).

Tips for Building Trust

Following are some tips for building the three types of student trust: trust in the teacher, trust in each other, and trust in themselves.

·   Nothing puts students into their alarm zone like feeling unwelcome. Make it clear from the first day that everyone is welcome, regardless of age, race, class, background, disability, or sexuality. If a student makes a prejudiced comment, even in passing, emphasize that your class is for everyone.

- The fear of making a mistake in front of the class keeps many students in their safety zone. Alleviate this fear by actively encouraging mistakes from the very beginning. I always tell students that if they're not making mistakes, they're not learning. Reward risk taking, not just success.
- Prepare less confident students. For example, warn them ahead of time that you will call on them so they have a good answer ready. When other students see a struggling peer succeed (and students quickly suss out each other's ability), they're more likely to take risks, too.
- Students may be reluctant to leave their comfort zone and try new activities, so model such things with gusto. Many of my ESL students had never sung in class before, so when we sang along to "California Stars" during our immigrant history unit, I made sure they saw me singing with 100 percent enthusiasm (if not talent).
- Pair activities and games are also good ways for students to build trust in each other. That's why teachers use them so much.

INTERVENE WITH STUDENTS WHO START (OR FALL) BEHIND

Have a plan and intervene early.

You'll know from the first day of class survey and error analysis which students are probably going to struggle in your class. As you collect data—from cold calling (see section later in this chapter), assignments, and assessments—you'll get a more specific idea of which students will need help to succeed.

It can be hard to intervene. I've certainly felt self-conscious telling students they weren't doing well. But I knew that if things didn't change, those students were going to fail. Intervening shows you care and think that there's still hope.

Few teachers intervene too much; most don't intervene at all. The trick is to do so early. If you wait too long, your student will accumulate too many deficits to be able to catch up.

Successful Interventions for Struggling Students

Here are some tips to help struggling students.

· Give them a handout with tutoring options and other learning resources.
· Set them up with more successful students as a tutors. (Give tutors extra credit, a thank-you card, or a glowing letter of recommendation for their trouble.)
· Encourage students to get into study groups, spending class time to form them if need be.
· Conference with each student individually, making conferences with struggling students longer and more in-depth.
· Communicate with struggling students more frequently, especially while working on a big project. (For example, have them e-mail you every week while they're writing their final paper.)
· Have an additional, optional prep class for everyone before the midterm or final, and strongly encourage your struggling students to come.

KNOW EVERY STUDENT'S NAME

Learn them early, learn them all, use them every class.

Knowing students' names is a little thing that makes a huge difference. It helps you check in with everyone, particularly the quiet students in back who are often the ones you need to check in with most. Being able to call on any student instantly is also important for nipping side chatter (or any other disruption) in the bud.

Don't assume that students know each other's names! Even if they've been sitting side by side for weeks, have them introduce themselves to one another at the beginning of the term and again when they do partner or group work.

Tips for Learning Names

Here are some time-tested tips for helping you remember students' names.

· Give students name tags to use on the first and second day.
· On the first-day student survey ask what names students prefer to go by in class.
· Make a map of where students sit in class; students usually sit in the same place every time.
· Use students' names every time you address them, at least until you remember them all.
· Pass back assignments by name so you can see which faces go with which names.

Hint: *It's good teacher practice to greet each of the students when they come in. (Teach Like a Champion refers to this as "Threshold" [Lemov, 2010, 197].) This is also a good opportunity to practice students' names.*

SHOW YOUR AGENDA

Some students need to see the map to get to the destination with you.

I write up my agenda on the board before each class. The agenda shows that you have a plan for the class. For some students, especially skeptical ones, this is crucial to reducing anxiety and persuading them to come along with you.

An agenda also helps you guide the class. If a student takes things off track, refer to the agenda to get the class back on track—especially if the student prematurely raises a topic that will be covered later that day. An agenda also provides accountability—if you don't get to something because you spent too much time on an earlier topic, your students know it. Alternately, you might give students the option to continue exploring the current topic at the expense of the next one. This gives more control to students, but may not be appropriate for all classes.

Finally, you can use the agenda to create suspense by putting a mystery item on it, marked only by a cryptic symbol. (For a short pop quiz I usually write "???" You might use it for something fun instead.)

> **Hint:** *Put your agenda in the same place every class. Students will instinctively look for it there.*

GOOD QUESTIONS ARE SHORT AND CLEAR

Same with instructions.

Questions are crucial to teaching. The following are some tips for coming up with good questions for classroom discussions, quick comprehension checks, or quizzes and tests.

How to Craft Good Questions

Here are some tips for crafting questions that maximize learning:

- Plan questions ahead of time and write them verbatim in your lesson plan. (These questions should be the basis of your quizzes and tests.)
- Alternately, begin by having students come up with questions they want to discuss.
- Make your questions short and specific.
- Avoid words like "most," "worst," and "definitely," which can intimidate students.
- Start with a broad question and then get more specific—or vice versa.
- Work up and down Bloom's Taxonomy: ask questions that test simple recall, comprehension, application, analysis, and so forth.
- If you improve a question or think of a better one, write it down and update your lesson plan that night.

How to Ask Questions

Following are some tips for asking questions:

- Ask one question at a time.
- Repeat your question verbatim if students don't understand it.
- If you need to change your question, start by making it more simple.
- Write your question on the board if you really want students to grapple with it.

Hint: Don't make students read your mind. If you ask the same question a few different ways and no one can answer it, check that the question doesn't have an amazingly specific answer that students can't be expected to produce. Better to *give them the answer and move on than to keep asking the question in more leading ways until someone finally says what you want to hear.*

Hint: *"Short and specific" works for instructions, too. Don't say, "I can't hear you, you need to speak up for us to hear you." Cup your hand to your ear and say, "Loud!" (With a smile, of course.)*

USE NONVERBAL COMMUNICATION

It's perfect for interventions and encouragement.

Nonverbal communication is amazing for quick interventions, because you can quickly communicate with an off-track student without distracting everyone else. I've used nonverbal communication successfully with students having side conversations (by making eye contact with them while continuing to lecture to the class) or who aren't doing the reading (by tapping my fingers on their desk while I walk around the room). This keeps students from feeling picked on while maintaining control of the class. To quote from *Teach Like a Champion,* "You want the intervention to be fast and invisible" (Lemov, 2010, 172). Sun Tzu would be proud.

Nonverbal encouragement works, too. When students ask a question, turn your whole body toward them, make eye contact, and smile. This shows you value students' input and models how you want students to treat one another.

> **Hint:** *Make sure your verbal and nonverbal communications are in harmony. When you ask a student a question, face him or her with your whole body to signal that you're paying attention to the answer. When you verbally encourage students to engage an activity, make your body language open and energetic.*

COLD CALL

It's a teacher's most powerful tool.

You run two risks when you ask students to raise their hands: either no one does, or the same few students as always do so yet again. Cold calling, the practice of calling on people who don't have their hands up, helps you avoid both problems.[2]

First, cold calling keeps the class moving. No more losing valuable minutes waiting for (different) people to raise their hands while listening to the sound of crickets. Second, you get to sample where your class is at. Instead of hearing from the same students who always get the answers right, you can ask questions of your two lowest students, two mid-level students, and then two of the highest-level students. If they all answer correctly, it's probably time to move on. (You can save the really challenging questions for the end, as a reward for those high-level students who've been waiting patiently to be called on.)

Cold calling is an effective way of showing you're in charge. You can even tell students that you're not taking hands or that they can raise their hands but that you're going to call on everyone. At first, this may be mistaken as punitive action. Indeed, most of us have had teachers who mistakenly used cold calling that way. But students will understand it isn't punitive when they see you

110

using it in every class and on every student—perhaps literally calling on every student every class. That's how I cold call.

There are several ways to take advantage of cold calling. You can scaffold, starting with easier questions and building from there. (These questions can be written ahead of time.) You can also base your questions on previous students' answers ("What do you think about John's answer, Mary?") so that students must listen to—and respect—one another's contributions.

Hint: A good trick is putting the student's name at the end of the question, so that each individual student must mentally answer the question you ask ("What's the difference between a compound and complex sentence . . . Ivan?"). The flip side is deliberately putting the student's name first if they need a bit more time to come up with the answer.

Hint: Never cold call randomly. Look for students making eye contact with you (they don't have the courage to raise their hand but want to try), students avoiding eye contact (engage them, too!), students who haven't spoken recently, students in all quarters of the room, students of different ages or countries of origin, and so on.

EFFECTIVELY DEAL WITH DIFFICULT STUDENTS

Do it for your class and for yourself.

It only takes one student to sabotage an entire class. That student can fracture the container you've built to keep students safe, undermine your authority to set the agenda, or encourage other

111

students to cheat on tests. Although few people are difficult on purpose, dealing effectively with difficult students is your responsibility.

How do you deal with bad behavior? First, by preventing it. If you cultivate your teacher persona, it will discourage students from acting up in the first place. Second, by planning activities well and switching them up as needed. A class that moves between teacher-centered and student-centered activities, which flows from lecture to group work to writing and other activities, which is focused on students' short- and long-term needs, will keep students more engaged, and less likely to disrupt what's providing value to them.

When students act up anyway, keep the following tips in mind.

How to Deal with Difficult Students

○ *Never attack the student.* Model how to deal respectfully with those who act disrespectfully. After all, just because this one student questioned a new activity, or said something homophobic, doesn't mean that other students didn't have the same thoughts. By addressing this person courteously you show that the class is (still) a safe place for everyone to learn. It also demonstrates your confidence.

○ *Listen and validate.* Listen to the student with your whole body. Don't roll your eyes or cross your arms. Let the person say his or her piece (within reason) and, if possible, validate the concern: "It sounds like you're frustrated with the pace of class. I'm definitely feeling tired after ninety minutes of class tonight. Is anyone else feeling tired?"

○ *Consider the complaint.* This is particularly challenging if it's not put forth as constructive criticism. I once had a student go off about how a workplace harassment quiz was unfair, even

112

though it covered material we had gone over repeatedly. In his tirade he mentioned how none of the quiz questions were in the class handouts. That night I made a handout that not only helped students learn the material but helped clarify what turned out to be my own disjointed understanding of the topic.

○ *Don't defend the activity.* George Lakey (2010, 176) points out how students often resist the activities they need the most. If a student who needs to analyze reading better complains about a reading activity, you can say something like, "Students in the past have said they got a lot out of this. If it doesn't work for you we have different activities coming up after it." A good learning activity proves its own worth.

○ *Encourage different forms of participation.* Sometimes students resist an activity because they can't do it your way. An exercise where students must repeatedly stand, write something on the board, and sit back down again may be excruciating for someone with a chronic injury. They may attack the activity rather than make their weakness known. Think of multiple ways students can participate—for example, by having students work in teams and letting a volunteer from each team write up all their answers.

○ *Allow an opt-out.* Give students a graceful opportunity to opt out of high-stakes activities. For example, I was once taught that, when doing a check-in, you should give people two possible questions to answer, like "Name a bad experience you've had in school OR name your favorite comic book villain, and explain why."

○ *Create a pressure valve.* Students need a chance to vent. In addition to formative assessments, encourage students to give you constructive criticism in private journaling exercises or as an occasional whole-class activity.

○ *Draw a line.* Know what you will never allow in class. You can refer to the code of conduct in the syllabus or just name the problem behavior in the moment. If you're caught off-guard, it's fine to address the behavior at the end of an activity, or at the end of class. Whatever you do, focus on the behavior, not on the student.

Story: You might think it's hard for me to think of the worst student I've ever had. It's actually about as hard as naming the best person who ever played for the Chicago Bulls.

I'll call this student "Imani." Imani never got through a class without belting out something horribly sexist or homophobic. His offensive comments were like a shock jock's best-of reel. While analyzing a case study of a man who said a workplace that openly accepted gays and lesbians violated his religious freedom as a Christian (Peterson vs. Hewlett-Packard Co., 2004), Imani opined, "WAS HE GAY? BECAUSE YOU HAVE TO BE AT LEAST A LITTLE GAY NOT TO LIKE LESBIANS."

I used the techniques above to deal with each individual instance of Imani's poor behavior. But I failed to prevent his misbehavior from repeating again and again. I was in denial about how bad he was until I looked back at my journal entries about the class while preparing the midterm. They seemed to focus a lot on Imani. But because he was older than I, and probably because he was also black and working class, I never did more than reprimand him for the latest unacceptable thing he said—and apologize to the one woman in the class after he said something exceptionally sexist. (She and the other students I spoke with privately insisted that they weren't too worked up about his comments.)

So how do you deal with a student like Imani? I still don't know. But if I ever see him on my roster again, I'll tell my administrators that, if he acts the same way, I'll quit before keeping him in the class.

DO IT AGAIN

Reflect, revise, repeat.

It's happened to all of us. You think of a great new activity that's perfect for the day's objective. But it's a disappointing, time-wasting, even soul-crushing failure in the classroom. Here's the secret: if something doesn't work, do it again as soon as possible.

First reflect on the activity and identify what went wrong. Was your explanation unclear? Were the goals too abstract or ambitious? Your reflection will help you create better activities in the future, even if this particular one doesn't pan out.

You might be hesitant to repeat an activity because you're afraid to stress out your students. But repeating unsuccessful activities (with changes) is actually less stressful than doing new thing after new thing—or repeating the same old things over and over again. I personally tell my students when I'm trying something new. They cut me some slack, help out more, and become active agents in their own learning.

Sometimes a previously successful activity will fail badly with different students. The same rules apply. Reflect on it, change it, and do it again.

"Too many people spend too much time trying to perfect something before they actually do it. Instead of waiting for perfection, run with what you've got and fix it as you go."
—Paul Arden, *Advertising Legend* (2006, 53)

115

TAKE BREAKS

Just because you're teaching doesn't mean they're learning.

Most teachers don't take enough breaks because we're afraid we won't cover everything that we need to. This reveals one of the fundamental paradoxes of our profession: the class is never long enough for the teacher, but is always too long for the students (this is true for each individual class as well as for the whole semester).

We should all probably take more breaks. Learning, after all, isn't what we do in front of the classroom, it's what happens in the minds of our students. If they're tired or distracted they won't be learning, even if they're physically present in class.

Break!

Here are some tips for helping students make the most of their breaks:

- Put the break halfway through class—that's when energy dips most.
- Before the break starts, write on the board what time you expect students back.
- Give students enough time to do something meaningful, like go to the soda machine or have a cigarette. (I generally give them ten to fifteen minutes.)
- Use the first or last few minutes to give one-on-one help to a student who's been struggling.
- Give students a two-minute warning before break is over.

116

- Pay attention to who comes back early (often students who are more eager) and who comes back late (often students who are less invested in class or who are pissed off at you).
- Gently chastise students who come back late to build in accountability.

Note: *In my three-hour evening classes I was unable to let my students have an official break. Instead, I'd lead them through a two-minute stretch at the halfway mark that left all of us refreshed.*

TIME TO LEAN, TIME TO CLEAN

Don't rest by default.

Teaching is tiring. It's hard to maintain focus on your students, your activities, and your objectives for an hour (or two, or three). It's easy for the teacher to zone out while students do group work or reading. Don't zone out. There's a checklist full of things you can do while students work.

Having said that, it's OK to rest—just make sure you do it on purpose. Toward the end of his training career, George Lakey scheduled his weekend-long facilitation trainings with a Saturday afternoon activity where students videotaped themselves facilitating a discussion. George revealed to us the next morning (in the section on planning long workshops) that he spent that time taking a nap so that he could keep things going until 9 or 10 p.m. Saturday night. He planned the day based on student needs, as the activity was extremely helpful, as well as his own.

While Students Work . . .

Here are some tasks to keep you productive while students are working, which should be often:

- Clear the board or take down any butcher paper.
- Walk around the room.
- Answer students' questions.
- Check for comprehension: ask questions, look at students' work, listen in on conversations . . .
- Recalculate the times for the remaining activities on your lesson plan.
- Grade quizzes or check homework.
- Prepare the next activity: retrieve handouts, take out any props, buffer videos . . .
- Make notes on different students' progress.
- Make notes on your syllabus and materials.
- Catch up on your paperwork: attendance, time sheets, grade sheets . . .
- Tidy up the room for the next teacher.

Hint: When you find yourself flustered and running around, it's usually a sign you're not taking advantage of student work time—or that the class is too teacher-centered.

YOU WILL GET BORED FIRST

Look for Mr. Miyagi moments.

The beginning of a course often feels boring to teachers. Our natural inclination is to rush to the good stuff at the end. But if you don't set the foundation at the beginning of the course, your students won't be able to make sense of your overall course objectives.

Notice when you feel bored. Are your students bored, too? If so, are they still learning? Are you upset because students aren't learning—or because you're not the fascinating center of attention?

If you get bored a lot, it's probably because you've mastered the mechanics of teaching, something that used to take all your focus. Congratulations! Now you get to focus instead on how students engage with what you present them. This takes more energy than teaching on autopilot and feeling bored, but it's some of the best learning you'll do.

Finally, if your students are getting bored a lot, show how the boring stuff is meaningful. In *The Karate Kid*, Daniel-san was POed that he was spending all his time doing manual labor for Mr. Miyagi.[3] At the height of his frustration, his sensei showed him how the same motion used for waxing a car could block an opponent's attack. Daniel suddenly realized that all the time he thought he was wasting on custodial work was powerful training for his upcoming karate tournament (which he won).

Daniel's sensei turned a potential breaking point into a breakthrough. If you pay attention, you'll find Mr. Miyagi moments everywhere. Guiding just one student through it can inspire an entire class.

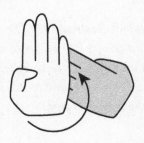

YOU WILL BIAS FOR THE HIGHEST

Half your students are below average.

As a teacher, you will naturally believe that your best students represent the average progress of all your students. This happens because you want students to do well and because you want to believe that you're a good teacher.

One way we teachers trick ourselves is by explaining away students' wrong answers and focusing on correct ones—usually from more advanced students. To borrow from *Teach Like a Champion* (Lemov, 2010), you ask the class "What was the 'restoration' in the 'Meiji Restoration'?" One student says a restoration of the military, a second says a restoration of Japanese power, and a third, strong student, says a restoration of the emperor to the throne—the correct answer. You might form a narrative that the class was collectively remembering what they had learned. But really, all you know is that two out of three students you called on got it wrong.

You hear disproportionately more from better students and disproportionately less from struggling ones, who generally keep a low profile. Make sure you listen to all your students—not just the ones who volunteer the right answers.

> **Note:** *This is like President Bush and WMDs in Iraq—when you arbitrarily pick and choose from a lot of different data, you'll always confirm what you already believe. When you find yourself unexpectedly progressing to advanced material, take a moment to make sure everyone really gets it.*

120

SURPRISE! IT'S A BIG CLASS

Make a few adjustments and you'll be fine.

Sometimes you'll end up with a huge class. This is great. You can reach more students than usual, and it's an opportunity to stretch your teaching skills. It can also be stressful because it almost always happens by surprise.

There are two things you can do to guarantee that your surprise big class goes well. First, take a deep breath and exhale. It's gonna be okay. Second, give your students a task (such as discussing the previous class with a partner) and spend a few minutes revising your lesson plan. For example, you'll want to do fewer (or no) activities where students have to walk around the class to get in groups.

It's natural to assume students are comfortable with the big class—as if they organized a flash mob with the express purpose of putting you on the spot. But they'll be just as surprised as you are. What's worse, they'll assume that you expected it!

Big classes can feel alienating to students. To minimize that alienation, the bigger the class is, the more important group work becomes. The trick is to have group work with minimal student movement. Pepper your lectures with activities such as having students talk about the material with a partner, or asking quick yes-or-no questions, or asking for a show of hands ("Raise your hand if you believe 'x'! Now raise your hand if you believe 'y'!"). Or have students form groups of four with those students sitting around them to discuss what they want to learn about today—if only once, at the beginning of class.

Speaking of lectures, big classes lend themselves to 'em because they take the same time to deliver no matter how many students are listening. But beware that big groups often have more questions. Keep a close eye on the clock when teaching big classes.

121

SURPRISE! IT'S A SMALL CLASS

Make a few adjustments and you'll be fine.

Small classes rock. You have more freedom in the activities you choose and get to know your students better. Yet a small class can feel awkward, to students and the teacher. Take the following three steps to succeed with a surprisingly small class.

First, take a deep breath and exhale. It's gonna be okay. Second, spend a few minutes revising your lesson plan to make the most out of your small class. Third, tell students how happy you are to have this unexpected opportunity. Make it clear that not only is this not a disappointment but a rare chance to go more deeply into the subject. You can also use this opportunity to answer specific questions or take requests.

There are more activities you can do with a small class, because it's easier for students to get out of their chairs and into various types of groups. If you planned for students to talk to a neighbor about the homework, now you can specifically pair them up with different types of thinkers or students with different opinions (concrete with abstract, Republican with Democrat).

You can also change a lecture to a discussion-based activity, because small classes ask fewer questions, and you therefore won't have to worry about not having enough time to cover everything. As a result, a small class is an opportunity to show students your more spontaneous side. (This is what makes a senior seminar so much more engaging than a survey course.)

Finally, a small class lets you tailor your teaching to the specific students in the room. It's a great opportunity to find out exactly where each of your students is and help them get to the next level.

Hint: Don't go on and on about how you were expecting more people to show up. This will just create the alienation of a big class with the awkwardness of a small one. Wait a couple minutes to let any stragglers come in and then go for it.

ENJOY THE GOOD TIMES

They get you through the bad times.

If you teach long enough you become something of a connoisseur of bad classes. Some sink slowly like the Titanic; others explode like the Hindenberg. Students may punish you with devastating criticism or withering silence. You can leave class feeling like a villain, an oaf, or a fraud.

So enjoy those good classes when you can. If things go really well, if the whole room engages a meaty topic or a lone struggling student finally gets a challenging concept, take a moment to let it sink in. These parcels of bliss are what get you through a trying career.

You can even take a moment to share this noticing with the class. Part of being a novice student is not recognizing when things are bad. (See Chapter 9, "Most students don't recognize bad teaching.") Novice students may not fully appreciate a good class, either. It's entirely appropriate, emotionally and educationally, to point out when something went well.

Maybe no one told your students it's OK to for them to get excited about a conversation topic. Or maybe you've unwittingly signaled that it's more important to finish group work on time than to get caught up analyzing a provocative idea. Either way, if

123

you explicitly identify how a class is going well, it's more likely to happen again in the future.

Just focus on how it was due to students' work and participation, so they don't mistakenly believe that good classes are entirely due to your efforts.

> **Note:** *There's a lot of magic during your first-ever course. Don't ever take your own happiness for granted—even (or especially) when you're just getting started.*

NOTES

1. For "Build trust to maximize learning," special thanks to Hannah Strange, and to George Lakey's *Facilitating Group Learning*. Lakey and others refer to the practice of deliberately building trust to maximize student learning as "building the container."
2. The cold calling chapter in *Teach Like a Champion* is comprehensive and amazing.
3. Props to teacher and friend Mark Trushkowsky for telling me about Mr. Miyagi moments.

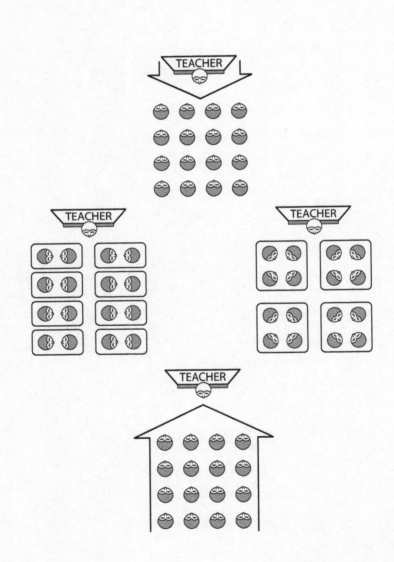

CHAPTER 7

How to Present Information

USE BLUE AND BLACK MARKERS

Use yellow and white chalk.

The same teachers who spend hours choosing the right font for their handouts may not give any thought to how they write on the whiteboard. But the text you write on the board is just like a handout. Students have to read it, copy it down, and refer back to it to promote their learning.

Tips for Effective Board Work

Use these tips to have the best board work around:

· Use black and blue markers (or yellow and white chalk) for text.

- Save red and green for "embroidery"—arrows, boxes, and so on.
- Make your letters big enough to be seen from the back of the class.
- Be consistent in labeling your titles and headings (<u>underlined</u> or in ALL CAPS—or <u>BOTH</u>
- For a long list, alternate between blue and black ink so the items don't run together.
- If you don't have a board, you can use butcher paper and masking tape (which comes off without leaving any residue).
  - Layer two pieces of butcher paper to prevent ink bleeding through to the wall.
  - Save butcher paper with important notes to bring home or to put up again in future classes.
- To help students study at home, write on the board the same way you want them to write your text down in their notes.
  - Check on students' note taking while walking around.
- Put text in your lesson plan the same way you want it on the board, verbatim. This will always be more concise than what you produce off the top of your head during class.
- You can still improvise! If you do think of a better way to communicate your idea, make a note of it in the moment and update your lesson plan when you get home.
- All these rules also apply to PowerPoint presentations.

Hint: Always have a spare dry-erase marker on you. They can go dry unexpectedly, and it's terrible being caught without one. Think of it as your teacher Epi-Pen.

LECTURES ARE BULLETPROOF

But lecturin' ain't easy.

Unlike group work or field trips, when it comes to lectures everything is under your control. As long as you have a room and a voice, you can lecture to forty students as easily as to four hundred.

Done correctly, lectures efficiently transmit information to students and effectively demonstrate your passion for the subject. Done incorrectly, a lecture can be as boring as C-SPAN and twice as deadly.

Preparing Your Lecture

Following are some tips on making the most of your lectures.[1]

- Is a lecture appropriate? Lectures are made to introduce much new information quickly.
- Have a point to make. Know what concepts you want to communicate to students.
- Start with a hook. Tell students what you'll cover and why they should care.
- Be excited. Include something genuinely exciting you: an anecdote, an experiment, or a mystery (Davis, 2009, 139).
- Keep it short. A lecture should generally be five to ten minutes long.
- Signpost. Verbally cue transitions ("and then," "however") and lists ("first," "second," "third," "last") (Davis, 2009, 143).
- Use visuals. Write on the board, pass around props, show charts, photos, or short videos, and so forth.
  - Visuals reduce teacher talk time, engage students, and better promote learning.

Lecture Like a Champion

The following tips will make your lectures more helpful for your students.

- Never read your notes verbatim. Refer to an outline and make eye contact with students.
  - Alternatively, you can lecture without notes to keep yourself on your toes and make sure you're not giving the same lecture year after year (Brinkley et al., 2011, 42).
- Pause occasionally, to give students a moment to catch up, or to pique their interest (Davis, 2009, 154).
- Look for signs of puzzlement or dismay (or sleep).
- If you use PowerPoint, never read your slides verbatim to your class. So. Boring.
- Warn students when you're about to cover something complicated so they'll be ready to think hard about it (Davis, 2009, 158).
- Break from the lecture. If you see students struggling, pause for questions or have them do an activity together, such as talking with partners to see if they've discovered anything they disagree with.
  - Incorporate solo, pair, or group activities into a longer lecture to keep students engaged.
- Change your lecture on the fly, if need be.
  - If students ask questions more basic than you expected, dial down the complexity so they don't get lost.
  - If students are better informed than you expected, take the lecture further or finish early.
- Summarize. Recap the main points before ending your lecture and taking questions.

"The hallmark of the great lecturer has always been the power to provoke, and there is no reason to think this power diminished."
—Andrew Delbanco, Scholar (2012, 63)

SHORTER IS BETTER

The more time you need to explain something, the less you understand it.

When you need a few paragraphs to verbally explain a concept to your students, you probably don't understand it as well as you ought to. Rehearse your lectures—even short ones—beforehand. The more you practice them, the shorter they will get, because practice helps you get to the heart of what you're trying to communicate. (This is similar to shortening a handout from three pages to two. You focus on what's crucial and cut the rest.)

A good teacher can quickly explain something several different ways. To explain the concept of the subject of a sentence to a beginning ESL student, you could say: "The subject is the noun that is usually at the beginning of a sentence," or "It's the noun that is doing the verb action in the sentence," or "In this sentence, it's 'My neighbor' who 'is reading the newspaper.'" The shorter your explanations, the more you can offer to struggling students.

FACILITATE DISCUSSIONS

Because good class discussions don't happen by themselves.

One of the best things about teaching adults is engaging in rich, nuanced conversations with people from all different

131

backgrounds. But this almost never happens by itself. You're quite likely to ask what you think is a provocative question and be met by deafening silence. As with so many things, a successful class discussion is usually the result of good planning and judicious intervention.

Perhaps the worst mistake with a class discussion is just letting it peter out. End a hearty discussion with a reflection activity, such as students writing a paragraph summarizing what they learned, or having small groups come to consensus on what point made during the class discussion was most important.

Tips for Facilitating a Good Discussion

Following these tips will help you facilitate a good discussion anywhere:

- Begin by looking at the day's objective. This will help you guide the conversation.
- Start the conversation with a specific question or two, written on the board if need be.
- Or begin by making the previous class's homework to bring in a juicy question, and then beginning class with students' questions (Davis, 2009, 100).
- "Prime the pump" by giving students a chance to engage the question individually (in a free writing exercise or quiet minute of contemplation) or in conversation with a partner before going to whole class discussion.
- Wait for answers. Wait until it's excruciating, and then wait even longer.
- Don't always call on the first hand raised—especially if it's one of the students who always raise their hands first.
- Don't respond to every comment, or you'll speak as much as your entire class put together.

132

- When a student asks you a question, have another student answer it—or ask it right back to the student who first asked the question.
- Go from concrete questions that check specific knowledge to abstract ones that force students to generalize from what they've learned so far. Switch between them as needed.
- If a student goes on and on, or starts going way off topic, it's your responsibility to politely but firmly cut them off.
- It's also your responsibility not to call on people who constantly raise their hands. I ask students who speak often to "step back," and encourage students who rarely speak to "step up."
- When discussion flags, play devil's advocate to provoke a response.
- When someone says something that contradicts an earlier statement, point it out. Sharpen the conflict to make the discussion more meaningful and lively.
- If a student says something you didn't understand, or if you space out and don't catch the statement, ask another student to rephrase it for the class.

USE THE VOCABULARY OF YOUR FIELD

Vocabulary is the coin of the realm.

In preparing your class, decide what vocabulary students should know by the end of it. For an English class, it may be grammar terms or genres of writing; for a yoga class, it may be the Sanskrit names of specific poses. Write out these terms along with concise definitions for them as a reference for yourself.

Then use this vocabulary in your lectures and writing, and make students do so, too. This will be reinforced when students do authentic reading from the field and when you test them on it.

Hint: One of the key points in learning vocabulary is understanding the difference between two related words. Think about the distinction between "cup" and "mug," or "chair" and "seat." Periodically ask students to distinguish between related vocab terms in your field.

MODELING IS POWERFUL

Even (other) animals do it.

Modeling—physically demonstrating what you expect students to do—is the basis of many forms of education, particularly in the physical arts. It's the primary mode of instruction in settings as varied as culinary schools to Marine Corps basic training.

The most influential model in the classroom is the teacher. You already model courtesy to your students and other classroom behavior norms. You should also model academic norms when you properly cite sources in your handouts and presentations. If you teach a physical skill, you model best practices with the safety equipment you use and procedures you follow while demonstrating techniques to the class.

Some students learn from modeling more than from abstract instruction. Even for students who are OK with the abstract, modeling is a great complement to text- or lecture-based teaching.

How to Model

Here are a few ways to use modeling in your classroom:

- Model a process while verbally describing it.
- One by one, list the individual steps in a process and then model those steps.

134

- Model a process silently and then verbally break it down.
- Model an action a few times and have students identify all the steps in the process.
- Model once, show the final product, and have students recreate the process.
- Model a common error and have students identify it.
- Model mistakes students are making so that they can see what they're doing incorrectly. You may need to exaggerate their errors so they can see them. Tell them you're exaggerating so they don't get upset.

Note: *Some teachers model their thinking process out loud: "Hmm, 48 times 98. I'm thinking that's too difficult for me to solve in my head. But I see that 98 is close to 100, so I'm just going to multiply 48 times 100 to get a rough estimate of the correct answer." This seems like a great way for teachers to deconstruct their expertise. (See Chapter 3, "Break it down.")*

USE SOLO, PARTNER, AND GROUP WORK STRATEGICALLY

Different types of groups maximize different kinds of learning.

We all instinctively know that we need to alternate between solo, partner, and group work. Here are some tips on which formation to use when:

- *Solo work,* such as writing a reflection paragraph or filling out a worksheet, is good for making each student engage with new material. It also helps quieter students prepare for class discussion.

· *Partner work* is good for quickly starting conversations, especially those that may go a little deeper and where trust is more important.
· *Groups of four to five* are big enough for real problem solving but still small enough to prevent shy (or lazy) students from hiding. (I don't recommend groups larger than five for that reason.)
· *Whole-class work* is best suited for students sharing ideas and brainstorming. Much like solo work, this is good for starting an activity, ending one, or both.

Watching students' emotions will help you know when to switch things up. If, during your lecture, students are getting frustrated, bored, or they check out, it's probably time for group work. If, during group work, they start getting quiet or off-track, it's probably time for another whole-class activity.

Hint: Try to keep students with the same partners or small groups at the beginning of the term so that they can get to know each other. By the middle of term, rearrange them so they're in groups that are more stable and effective.

MAKE THE MOST OF GROUP WORK

We are most and least productive in groups.

Modern life revolves around collaboration. Whether it's group writing via Google Docs or using Facebook to organize a ski trip, we work with others now more than ever.

However, most of us were never taught how to work in groups. That makes it difficult for us to guide our students' group work. That's too bad, because groups are where students—where all of us—are either most or least productive.

Tips for Effective Group Work

Here are some tips to help your students get the most from their group work.

- Explain the task and goal(s). Write them on the board, if need be.
- Build in accountability. For example, tell each group beforehand that they will have to report their results to the class.
- If needed, make sure groups have roles assigned: note taker, timekeeper, facilitator, reporter (for the report back), and so forth. Check that these roles are filled or assign them yourself.
- For intentionally random groups, count off. (To get four groups, have students count off one to four, and then have all the "number ones" get together, and so forth.)
- For more personal groups, let students choose.
- For quick groups, have students work with the people right around them.
- Move students with impunity. If two students always get off-track when in the same group, switch one of them out before starting the activity.
- Walk around the room during group work to answer questions and keep everyone focused.
- Make time restraints clear and warn students when time is almost up.
- You can extend time if the conversation is juicy or shorten it to keep energy levels up.

Tips for Effective Report Backs

Report backs can be the best or worst part of group work. Follow these steps to make your report backs shine:

1. First, have each group report back just one thing, especially if they have generated a big list of items to report: adjectives, photography terms, ways to improve the class . . .
2. Write these items on the board—with another student helping, if need be—to keep things moving quickly.
3. After each group has reported their first thing, go around again and have each group report their second thing, and so on. (See Figure 7.1.)
4. Repeat until everything has been reported.
5. Engage in group analysis, whether it's identifying trends, common items, or unique ones.

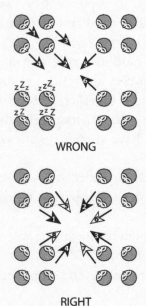

Figure 7.1 The wrong and right ways for groups to report back to each other

This method is far better than having the first group report back everything, and then having the next group report back everything, which is tedious for everyone. Feel free to try this in your next staff meeting!

INCORPORATE CURRENT EVENTS

The currenter, the better.

Engaging current event in class shows students how your course is relevant to their lives. It will also help you pay attention to your own everyday life, because everything you come across will be potential fodder for class. (ESL teachers constantly analyze new advertising slogans with students. "We usually don't make the present continuous out of stative verbs. So why does McDonald's say, 'I'm loving it'?")

It may be enough to simply acknowledge a current event at the beginning of class. I had a teacher-training workshop that met a few days after the war in Iraq started in 2003. The instructor, Dr. James Iler, began by thoughtfully asking, "Has the whole world really changed?" We didn't go into it, but by acknowledging what was on all our minds, he freed us to move on. (He also made it clear that he wasn't clueless.)

DON'T CORRECT EVERY MISTAKE

Knowing what to correct and when is the heart of teaching.

The number one thing students ask for is to have all their errors corrected. But no one really wants that. If you show students who thought they were doing OK that they're making myriad mistakes, they will go into their alarm zone, stop learning, and shut down.

Overcorrection causes underlearning. Undercorrection keeps students in their comfort zone. This is where your subject matter and teaching expertise are most crucial: to know the order in which students need to learn new ideas and skills in order to improve.

For example, a jujitsu sensei might see an intermediate student throw awkwardly and make a sloppy pin. But because generating power from the hips is the most important intermediate level skill (to keep students from straining their backs), the sensei would likely compliment the student on the throw and make one or two small suggestions to start ironing out the kinks. The sensei knows you can't correct subtle errors before the foundation is set.

On the other hand, black belts (senior students) might give the intermediate student a laundry list of corrections that will screw up the student's throwing form before it has settled. Those black belts might be excellent practitioners. They might even be able to beat up their own sensei! But they don't yet know how to use their expertise to help newer students build their own knowledge.

Correcting mistakes is the easy part. Knowing what not to correct is perhaps the greatest challenge in teaching.

ALWAYS TELL STUDENTS WHERE THEY ARE

Put "No Surprises" into practice.

If your class is graded (or otherwise formally evaluated), let students know where they are throughout the term. First, return all graded assignments in a timely manner, ideally in a week or less. As with tests, do not return assignments until you've made sense of students' performance on them.

Give students a status report early enough in the term for them to make up for a poor start. If they don't find out their grade

140

sucks until it's too late to improve it, why should they bother trying?

Telling students where they are may be even more important in nonacademic settings. With yoga or martial arts, give students feedback on their specific techniques and how they're doing overall. It's hard for practitioners, especially new ones, to discern their own progress.

NOTES

1. For "Lectures are bulletproof," thanks to *A Handbook for Adjunct/Part-Time Faculty and Teachers of Adults* by Donald Greive, EdD, and to *The Chicago Handbook for Teachers.*

CHAPTER 8

How to Develop Your Teacher Persona

THE CLASSROOM IS NOT A DEMOCRACY

But you can help prepare students for democracy.

Some teachers believe that the classroom should be a democracy. I disagree. A classroom can never be a democracy—and shouldn't be, either. Here's one reason: everyone in a democracy has equal rights and responsibilities. In the classroom, the teacher is far more responsible to the students than vice versa.

But there's another reason we can't make democracies of our classes. None of us knows what real democracy is like. Our government is beholden to a handful of wealthy corporations and limits our civic participation to pressing a button every few years. We have even less democracy at work, where employers dictate our working conditions and we can be fired for almost any reason or none whatsoever.

In my opinion, a real democracy gives people the power to make decisions about those things which affect them most. In a real democracy, a city or corporation couldn't put an incinerator into a poor community without the consent of the people who live there. More holistically, I think a democratic society gives all workers an equal voice in their workplace and all people an equal voice in their government.

Unless you grew up in rural Madagascar[1] you probably haven't experienced a democratic society. And if we've never known democracy ourselves, I don't think we can teach our students democracy by arbitrarily shoehorning participatory practices into our otherwise hierarchical classrooms.

It's best to acknowledge the truth: you're the boss. You'll learn from students and change the course to meet their needs, but you're the one in charge. That's not so bad. Far worse, I think, to pretend (or believe) that your class is a democracy when, in reality, it's one person telling everyone else what to do. We have enough of that already.

And besides, if you use formative assessments your class will probably be the most democratic your students have ever had. Even if it's really a benevolent dictatorship.

Which Country Is Your Classroom?

Below is a list of countries and the different types of teaching they correspond with. Which is yours?*

North Korea: A tyrannical regime led by a distant autocrat.

Classroom: A teacher who ruthlessly enforces arbitrary rules.

144

Japan: A corrupt democracy where most citizens still enjoy a good standard of living.

Classroom: A bad teacher who gives everyone an A.

Madagascar: A weak state where the people live mostly independent from the government.

Classroom: A teacher who gives suggestions to students who are free to take or leave them.

United States: A nominal democracy where corporate interests hold almost all power.

Classroom: A teacher who claims to listen to students but ends up doing whatever the administration says.

*Ideally, your class is like none of these countries!

YOU ARE THE LEADER IN THE CLASSROOM

"Management is doing things right; leadership is doing the right things."
—Peter Drucker, Business Guru (Covey, 1989, 101)

When I think about teaching in the abstract, I picture either an anonymous figure hunched over a lesson plan or Robin Williams in *Dead Poets Society*. That's the constant tension in teaching. We're expected to micromanage a myriad of classroom tasks and then inspire students to do them all.

√Being a good leader is difficult in any context. I will outline here three ways I think of the teacher as leader in the classroom.

Emotional Leader: Whether it's fear of taking risks, frustration with difficult tasks, or satisfaction from learning something new, emotions are central to learning. As teacher, you set the emotional tone for the class. Even the greenest teacher does this instinctively.

145

Improve your class by consciously setting the emotional tone your students need to maximize their learning.

Decider: Academics assumes that teaching consists of micromanaging the execution of your carefully laid plans. But teachers make in-flight corrections all the time. How do you decide which course objectives to prioritize when you realize your students won't accomplish them all? How do you look out for that one student who's way behind everyone else—and is becoming a target of classroom ridicule? Planning is important. But if you spend all your time on execution you will kill your class. Don't just manage—lead.

Role Model: You are a professional role model. You show students how you are engaged with your field, how you maintain and satisfy your intellectual curiosity, how you have a nuanced understanding of your field and are successful within it. You also model your understanding of your own limitations and how you deal with them.

Students don't expect you to be infallible. If they were asked, they'd say you were an ordinary person, just like them. However, to maximize their learning they have to believe (at least in the moment!) that you possess something that makes you different and better than who they are right now. After all, if taking your class won't make your students better people, why should they bother with all the hard work?

OWN THE ROOM

Or the room will own you.

Part of being in control of your class (in the service of maximizing learning) is showing that you're in control of its physical space.

The most obvious way to do this is to not get boxed in behind your desk at the head of the room.

Walk around the front of the room while lecturing, and walk around the whole room while students are doing individual or group work. This is a simple but effective way of establishing yourself as the teacher. It'll also help you catch student errors and prevent side chatter.

And if students leave their backpacks in the aisle, don't hesitate to (politely) ask them to move them. In addition to letting you walk through the class without breaking your neck, this is a subtle way to show that you're in charge.

YOU ARE NOT A SOCIAL WORKER

Their job is even harder than ours.

After a few years of teaching, I thought I knew how to handle everything. Then I had a woman walk into class with a black eye. I had no idea what to do.

With the best of intentions, some teachers do amateur social work. They try to solve students' workplace, family, or personal problems. This is tempting, but a huge disservice to that student, yourself, and the rest of your class. It's hard to be a social worker, and it's hard to be a teacher. If you try to do both you'll do neither well. Instead, you'll end up giving mediocre advice to students who need serious help and not put enough energy into the class you're supposed to be teaching.

A good compromise is having a list of resources on hand at the beginning of the term. These can include government agencies and nonprofits that provide mental health and medical services. It may be a lot of work to collect this information, but it's still easier than becoming a social worker. God bless 'em.

> **Hint:** *A happy exception is when a student has a specific problem that relates to what you're doing in class, or that affects many students. For example, if you're talking about communicating clearly and a student is having miscommunications with their boss, it's appropriate to address this in class.*[2]

DISCLOSE THOUGHTFULLY

Tell students about yourself when it serves their learning.

I used to keep myself a blank slate to my students. I thought that talking about what challenged or excited me was an act of narcissism that distracted from my teaching. *Mentor,* by Laurent Daloz, changed my mind. Daloz (2012) explains the importance of mentors' talking to students about where they are on their personal journey. (See Chapter 1, "Find out where the student is on his or her journey.")

Now I think that thoughtfully telling students about yourself is crucial to maximizing learning. Of course you should tell students what you love about your field. This is, at the very least, a good hook. Over time, as you learn about your students, show how you share their problems, and how learning the subject has helped you become the person you want to be. For example, martial arts instructors may talk about how learning self-defense skills gave them the confidence they had always wanted.

Blabbing about yourself to a captive audience is still an act of narcissism. But withholding who you are from a group of people who have made themselves vulnerable to you can be a kind of domination.

> **Note:** *Stephen Brookfield (2013) notes that starting a class by disclosing how much you have struggled with the field can be especially inspiring to struggling learners.*

WHEN YOU DON'T KNOW, SAY "I DON'T KNOW"

But first ask students if they know the answer.

One of the best things about teaching adults is your class will always know way more than you do. That means they'll sometimes ask a question you don't have the answer to.

Here's the oldest trick in the book. Ask the same question back to the whole class. Someone is bound to have at least an insight into it. In fact, the person asking the question usually has some thoughts on the matter, if not the whole answer itself. Try asking something like, "What do you think? If you did know the answer, what would it be?"

If that still doesn't work, say "I don't know." Most adults can recognize BS. When you acknowledge that you don't know the answer to a difficult question, they'll respect the hell out of you. (Besides, students often ask questions they know don't have pat answers.)

The key to using "I don't know" is to tell them you'll find out—and then find out. If the question is at all relevant to the class, write it down, find out the answer and bring it back the next class. This shows you care about your students' questions and not just your own.

Story: In college, I once had to go to the office of the great environmental studies professor Karl Jacoby to request the course code for his urban ecology class. I asked if he could recommend any popularly written books on urban planning like *The Geography of Nowhere,* which I had just finished. Dr. Jacoby looked startled and said, "I can't think of any." Then again, to himself, as if in a trance, "I can't think of any . . ."

I returned the next day for my course code. Right before I left, he said, "Oh, and one more thing," and rattled off the names of ten accessible books on urban planning. Dr. J. ended up being one of the best professors I ever had.

BE IN CONTROL

A good teacher knows and controls everything.

A teacher's scarcest resource is student attention. To make the most of it you must be in control. Of as much as you possibly can.

Control begins with the lesson. Know what activities you'll do, how long they will take, and how to explain and assess them. Make sure you have all the handouts, dry-erase markers, and other materials you'll need.

Next, control how students engage these activities. To foster an environment where they'll take risks and collaborate, you must know your students' names, abilities, interests, histories, and friendships with one another. Comprehensive knowledge of your students is key to maximizing control of the class and, therefore, student learning.

150

Finally, make your control look effortless. You're not really in control if you react to every little surprise. That's the power of laughter. It shows the unexpected doesn't faze you.

BE SPONTANEOUS

Spontaneity is the complement of control.

If the control model of teaching assumes scarcity, the spontaneity model assumes abundance—an abundance of opportunities to help students learn and grow. Fear, frustration, and judgment keep us from recognizing these opportunities.

Don't panic when class deviates from your plan. Are students not doing your activity because they've mutinied against you or because they're focusing on something else they need to practice more? When students get upset, should you rush past it or explore more deeply what might be a serious problem?

If you focus only on control you'll miss the (many) times when students tell you something you need to hear. When you find the balance between controlling as much as you need to and being open to everything else, teachable moments will manifest everywhere.

Too much control stifles spontaneity. Having open space in your lesson plans gives you the room to be spontaneous. If your lessons aren't planned down to the last second, then when students come in with a burning question or specific problem, you have time to engage it. This is key to making classroom learning connect to your students.

> *"A good detective tries to know everything. But a great detective knows just enough to see him through to the end."*
> —Jedediah Berry, *The Manual of Detection* (2009, 240)

WHEN YOU GET UPSET, CHECK YOUR EXPECTATIONS

These are some of your best learning opportunities.

Moments of intense frustration or keen disappointment are common in teaching. Don't despair! It's probably due to being emotionally invested in something going your way, rather than focusing on maximizing learning.

In the moment, recognize your frustration or disappointment for what it is, find its source, and approach it with curiosity instead of judgment. Strong emotions are closely tied to powerful learning. Moments of teacher pain can be some of your best learning opportunities if you treat them as such.

Regardless of how frustrated you are, it's probably not as bad as you think. Your students might not even notice what you think is a terrible failure.

Story: I spent the beginning of my career in Oakland's Chinatown. I remember one class where my students were mispronouncing "dollar." After a few repetitions and increasing frustration on my part, I had two epiphanies. One, they weren't going to get past "dohr-rar" today, and two, that wasn't so bad. A native speaker could still understand what they meant.

After my realization, we switched to a different activity and went on to have an amazing class. (I later found out accent is one of the last things people learn—and among the least important.) The problem wasn't my students' pronunciation but my own hang-ups about Asian accents.

DON'T GET PISSED OFF

The class is about your students—not you.

All of us are invested in our teaching, which is good. In the process, we often get invested in our particular materials, our lesson plans, and even the activities we choose, which isn't so good.

When things go pear-shaped, don't get pissed off. First, it keeps you from finding the best answers to the problem. Second, it's a sign of weakness. It shows that both you and your precious plans are as fragile as a shoe box full of porcelain mice.

Getting pissed off also communicates that your class is all about you and your happiness, which will make students focus on taking care of you rather than on their own learning. Finally, if the problem itself is anger—say, between two students who strongly disagree—your own anger will only exacerbate it.

SOMETIMES, GET PISSED OFF

You might have to get pissed off at your students once.

It's your job to push students into their discomfort zone. If their comfort zone includes not doing assignments or being lax about safety standards, it may be appropriate to use anger to help them unlearn those bad habits.

How do you know when it's appropriate to get pissed? Here are my standards: Was a rule broken? Was it serious? Did students know the rule existed? If these three standards are met, spell out your expectation of your students, how it was violated, and how that diminishes their learning or risks their safety.

One day in my writing class it appeared that almost no one had done the homework. I confirmed this was the case, asked for an amazing excuse, and then explained how badly this

153

compromised what they needed to know—for that day and the rest of the term. I told them how disappointed I was and ended class ten minutes early; literally every other class had gone up to the bell. The following day almost everyone had their homework. I've never had to use anger this way more than once a term.

It may also be appropriate to get pissed off when you're teaching a skill that's performed under pressure, like self-defense or first aid. Getting angry at your students can prepare them for working with adrenaline running through their veins. This is particularly true if you're preparing them to work with angry people. Just be sure you use your anger to further the goals of class—not to vent your frustration.

If you're using anger to teach students to work under pressure, save it for more experienced students and make sure they (and you) have a chance to collect themselves emotionally before leaving class. (Special thanks to sensei Mike Esmailzadeh, who notes that you shouldn't use this teaching tool when you're already angry.)

> **Note:** *Getting angry shows students that they have hurt your feelings. If they respect you at all they'll try to avoid doing so again in the future.*

ONE TEACHER

Because you're responsible for the class.

Probably most of us like teaching adults because we can share power in the classroom. This contrasts with typical K–12 classes where the teacher is the boss of the students. Having said that, you're still the one ultimately responsible for everyone's learning.

So if a student tries to take over the class, don't let it happen. The student may try to do so because of a sense that the class is getting out of control, which can work in very small doses. For example, a student might tell a neighbor to stop talking and stay on task. But there will be times when a student vocally tells you to continue an activity when it's time to move on, or tries to switch topics prematurely.

At those times I will simply tell the class what to do. If someone continues lobbying, I literally say, "One teacher today." I smile, but I'm not joking.

It's fine to ask students what they want to do, but it's your responsibility to decide what happens when. People sense weakness. When you're unable or unwilling to steer the class, someone else will steer it for you—and that person won't have the same understanding of where it needs to go. Be bold and confident in front of students; reflect on possible mistakes afterward. And apologize later if need be.

Many difficult students assert themselves immediately. From the first day of class they say wildly inappropriate things, such as insulting other students or criticizing your teaching. Don't let them. My technique is to look them in the eye and say, "That's not appropriate."

If it continues, explain how their behavior does not meet the expectations spelled out in your syllabus or class expectations, and that if that's a problem this may not be the class for them. Especially if it's early enough to withdraw for free, this is often enough for them to quit until they're ready to respect themselves and other students enough to be in a classroom environment. (You may want to pull them aside to have this conversation.)

Just one disruptive student can destroy the trust needed for real learning. For the benefit of your students and yourself, intervene with difficult students immediately.

> **Hint:** *Most of the difficult students I've had were too advanced for my class. They acted up because they were bored: by helping other students too often, answering every question, reading the newspaper during activities, and so on. Identify these students with your first-day survey and needs analysis. Make it clear that your class is not the right place for them—even if they want an easy A.*

BE DISOBEDIENT

"If you can't solve a problem, it's because you're playing by the rules."
—Paul Arden, Legendary Adman (2003, 49)

Teachers are a school's frontline enforcers. That's why we feel like cops so often. (Did a student arrive more than ten minutes late? Mark 'em absent!)

√There are times when you need to break a rule to do what's right by students. A solid mission statement is key to making sure you break rules for a good reason. (See Chapter 2, "Have a mission.") I've already said I won't pass a student who's not ready for the next level. But there are other rules I have happily broken.

At my old school, students absent for more than two weeks were forced to register all over again. This was a bean counter's move to coerce students into showing up more often and thus increase our revenue from the state—regardless of the fact that students typically missed class due to working overtime or taking care of their families. Forcing them to reregister was strictly punitive.

One time a student returned to class after a six-month absence. He'd been deported. A new student asked if he hadn't been gone too long to come back to class. So I asked the whole class, "Well, is two weeks too long to be absent?" ("No!")

I continued. "Is one month too long?" (Most said "No," with a few abstentions this time.) "Is two months too long?" (A few objections from newer students, while my old students knew what was coming.) "Is three months too long?" And so on, all the way up to six months, when I declared, "It's never too long to come back to class!"

Then I explained that although some people think that the students are there for the school, we knew that the school is there for the students—and as long as I was in the classroom they could always come back. It was a powerful ritual that reaffirmed our classroom culture of mutual support in the service of learning, not the heartless enforcement of arbitrary rules. When students saw that the six-months-absent student was welcome back, they knew that truly everyone was welcome in my class.

In the space of one generation, we have witnessed terrorist attacks at home and two major wars abroad. With that in mind, I'll close with three quotations on the topic of disobedience.

> *"As soon as you say the topic is civil disobedience, you are saying our problem is civil disobedience. That is not our problem . . . Our problem is civil obedience. Our problem is the numbers of people all over the world who have obeyed the dictates of the leaders of their government and have gone to war, and millions have been killed because of this obedience."*
> —Howard Zinn, Historian (Zinn and Arnove, 2009, 483–484)

157

"I obeyed. Regardless of what I was ordered to do, I would have obeyed. Certainly, I would have obeyed. I obeyed, I obeyed."
—Adolf Eichmann, Nazi (Von Land, 1983, 198)

"Resist much, obey little."
—Walt Whitman, Poet[3]

NOTES

1. Check out the works of anthropologist David Graeber for more about the fascinating case of ungoverned Madagascar. Tangentially, his book *Debt: The First 5000 Years* will be the best nonteaching book you read all year.
2. Thanks to Art Ellison for giving me this advice after reading a very early excerpt from this book.
3. From "Walt Whitman's Caution" (1860). The entire poem reads:

   > To The States, or any one of
   > them, or any city of The
   > States, <u>Resist much, Obey</u>
   > <u>little,</u>
   > Once unquestioning obedience,
   > once fully enslaved,
   > Once fully enslaved, no nation,
   > race, city, of this earth,
   > ever afterward resumes
   > its liberty.—

   Underlining in original. From the Walt Whitman Archive. http://whitmanarchive.org/manuscripts/transcriptions/amh.00009.html

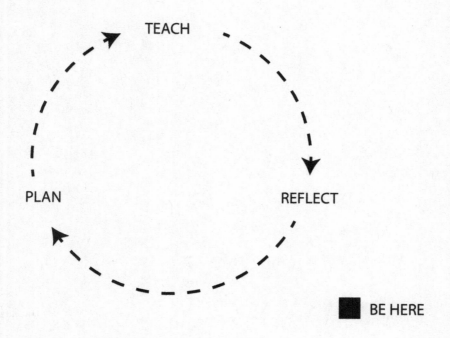

CHAPTER 9

Growing as a Teacher

SET YOUR OWN TEACHER OBJECTIVES

"By the end of the year, the teacher will be able to . . ."

It's important to consciously improve your teaching practice for two reasons. First, to teach better, and second, to not go crazy.

Our challenge is that the education system is too focused on student objectives. We need to consciously develop our own teacher objectives. My great ESL instructor friend Mike Missiaen (mih-SHAWN) taught me the importance of setting explicit objectives for yourself.

I'll give you a common example. If you're a new teacher, you spend too much time lesson planning. That's because you're still figuring out how long activities take and in what order to put them. But if you continue to spend one hour planning for every hour that you teach, you will burn out. So a useful goal for almost every new teacher is, "Teacher will be able to spend only forty-five minutes planning for every hour taught." Over the years you can reduce this to thirty minutes per hour or less.

We know that, for novice students, learning to learn is as difficult as learning any particular topic. Same goes for teachers. Learning to grow—finding out what resources even exist and which ones work for you—is at least as difficult as learning any particular teaching skill.

So set some goals and start learning to teach better—and more sustainably. The rest of this chapter will help you do so.

> **Note:** *Many teachers stay in character while they teach. I know I spent years in front of a classroom being preternaturally enthusiastic in the hopes of making students learn from me and love me. One of your long-term goals should be to closely match your teacher persona to your actual persona. This will make your job less exhausting. Today, my students find me a little less exciting, but I don't finish class feeling like a wrung-out dishcloth. (Thanks again, Mike!)*

LEARNING TO REFLECT WILL MAKE YOU YOUR OWN BEST TEACHER

Reflection is the most important part of teaching yourself.

The ability to learn from our own experience is among the most important skills anyone can develop. Reflecting on your teaching

162

practice makes every class you teach a learning opportunity. This is especially rich at the beginning of your career, when novel and challenging things happen all the time.

Sample Teacher Reflection Questions

Whether your process is writing in a journal, posting to your blog, or talking with colleagues after work, here are some questions to help you get the most out of your reflection:

- How did this activity or class match my expectations? Why?
- What contributed to this activity's success? The class's success?
- What was suboptimal? What went wrong? How could I improve it?
- What surprised me today?
- What have I learned from this experience that I can use in the future?

Hint: Don't forget to reflect on success! Doing so cultivates more of it. Never take success for granted.

MOST STUDENTS DON'T RECOGNIZE BAD TEACHING

And even if they do, they won't tell you.

We all want student feedback. But don't assume that students will necessarily tell you what's wrong. Many are too polite to give substantive criticism, or too intimidated by educational institutions and classroom power dynamics to openly criticize you.

Your students may never have had great instruction, or the last time they did was in grade school. They may confuse good teaching with the teacher being likable, or smart, or mean. If they fail, they're likely to blame themselves—not you, the materials you chose, your assessments, or the countless other choices that make up your teaching.

Adults tend to vote with their feet. If they don't like your class, they'll leave. (You'll see this most between the first and second day.) Having said that, most adult students who drop out do so due to work or personal obligations, not because of the teacher.

So don't assume you're bad just because students leave. But don't assume you're any good just because they stick around and don't complain.

THE WORST TEACHERS THINK THEY'RE AMAZING

How do you know that's not you?

All teachers think they're above average. There's only a 50 percent chance that's true for you, and it's faint praise, anyway.

The fact is that most teachers aren't very good. They may not be bad, but they're not very good, either. This includes me. I think, at best, I'm a good teacher. But I believe I'm on the path to becoming very good.

As far as I can tell, only a few teachers are truly bad. But all of them think that they're amazing. That's probably why they stop critically evaluating themselves; they don't even know that they need to improve.

Bad teachers also find ways to blame everything on their students. If their students all did lousy on a test, it's because they didn't study hard enough, or they're lazy, or they're stupid. (Never mind that the teacher is the one variable they all have in common.) If one student in their class does well it proves they're good teachers. (Even though there are always a few students who excel at everything they do.)

Being convinced that you're amazing means you're probably secretly terrible. If you can't accept the likelihood that you're not yet a great teacher, you're unlikely to ever become one.

IT'S HARD TO IMPROVE

Do it anyway.

It's difficult for adult education teachers to improve. It's rare that students or administrators tell us what we need to work on, and still more rare that we have the time or resources to do so. And even if we manage to improve, it seems we're just as likely to get fired as we were before.

But we still need to improve. In my experience, most teachers—most people—do one or two things well and everything else passably at best. If you're a beginning teacher, you're probably not even at that level yet.

There are many opportunities to become a better teacher, from reflecting on your practice to going to grad school. No matter what method you use, when you learn something new, integrate it ASAP. Present to your peers, post to your blog, and then change your practice accordingly. This will cement your new learning.

The challenge of improving is yet another reason to be active in the labor movement. It's only through collective organizing that we'll get the full-time positions and job stability we need to be able to focus on our own professional development. To put it another way, it's hard to be professionals when we're treated like temps.

/Opportunities for Improvement

The following professional development opportunities are available to every teacher (listed from least to most time commitment):

· Reflecting on your practice
· Recording and watching your own teaching
· Peer observation
· Reading journals or blogs in your field
· Individual study or peer study groups
· Applying for research grants
· Mentoring (with a lead teacher or peer)
· Collaborating with a trusted administrator
· Continuing education classes
· Attending conferences
· Presenting at conferences
· Publishing in your field
· Getting an advanced certification
· Going to graduate school

Note: *It's even more difficult for part-time teachers to improve. We're less likely to be eligible for professional development funds, we have more demanding schedules because we teach at two (or more) schools, or must work an additional unrelated job to pay the bills. It would be dishonest to ignore these structural disadvantages. But we must find a way to improve despite them.*

YOU ARE AN ENTREPRENEUR

Until you get tenure or marry rich, you're in business for yourself.

The state of teaching today is that you'll often have more than one job at a time, and rarely have any job longer than a couple years. This makes you an entrepreneur. The more you act like one the more likely you are to have teaching work.

How to Entrepreneur

Here are some tips for staying gainfully employed as a teacher.

· Create a professional e-mail account. Gmail looks the most professional and tech savvy.
· Create a LinkedIn profile and connect to your colleagues, present and past.
· Create a professional website with WordPress or another free service.
· Update your CV—and put it on your website!
· Post your best materials (only) on your website.
· Get letters of recommendation from former employers, colleagues, professors, and peers.
· Get testimonials from past students—especially if you work in a nonacademic setting.
· Build your personal network and never say no to lunch.
· Get a free Google Voice phone number to avoid giving your personal number to students.
· Take down incriminating Facebook pictures.
· Watch your taxes—especially if you work at two schools (they won't withhold enough) or if you're an independent contractor (pay your quarterly taxes!).

Note: *Although it makes me vomit in my mouth when I say it, the work you do builds your brand. Make sure your brand is something that students (and schools) want to buy.*

FOR-PROFIT SCHOOLS HAVE A LOT TO TEACH US

But they will never put academics first.

It's a cliché in adult education that we strive for student-centered learning. In many ways the private sector takes this more seriously than public schools. For example, private adult schools frequently use surveys to check for student satisfaction in a way that's unknown in public education. Private schools are also nimble where public schools are not, by continuously offering new classes and expanding existing ones on demand.

For-profit schools are also quick to close classes and fire teachers. As much as they care about academics (and many care a lot!) they care about profit more. In the private sector, the student is the customer. When there's a conflict between academics and customer satisfaction—such as when a student wants to promote to the next level before being ready—for-profit schools tend to act like any other business and put the customer first.

Public schools, by definition, are outside the free market. This is to the tremendous advantage of students' interests as a whole, even if it's to the disadvantage of any individual student. To wit: public school teachers can maintain the educational standards of the school by flunking students with impunity. In this regard, public schools know something that private schools may never be able to learn.

ADMINISTRATORS ARE PEOPLE, TOO

They might want our job, but we don't want theirs.

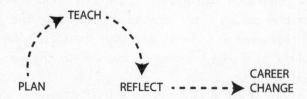

Administrator do many things, none of which we want to do. They fill out paperwork for teachers, for students, for the state, and for the institution itself. They make sure classes are filled with students, taught by teachers, cleaned by janitors, and kept whole by maintenance workers.

Don't assume administrators love education any less than you do. Many used to be teachers themselves! They exist to let us focus on classroom instruction. Unfortunately, we're generally only aware of them when they make a mistake. Unless you can honestly say, "I wish I had to fill out more paperwork," you have an administrator to thank.

Some of you reading this book will discover that, as much as you love education, you're not cut out for teaching. You are the ones who should become administrators.

A great administrator can help you become a better teacher, by giving you advice, changing your assignment to one for which you're better suited, or otherwise helping to cultivate your strengths. Here's a story from David Lazerson, a special education teacher in the Florida public schools. Among other accomplishments, he's been inducted into the National Teachers Hall of Fame for his work using music to teach kids with disabilities.

My use of music did not really start as a conscious decision. I just happened to bring my guitar to school one time, and I was just doing some kid songs with them, and I had passed out some percussion instruments. These were teenage students with profound autism. They responded pretty well. The principal happened to come by and later she said, "Wow. That was the only time I've seen so many really engaged in a group activity."

So I started doing music every day, and pretty soon other teachers in the school start bringing their kids by for music. The principal then said that she wanted to start doing music for the whole school, so we set up the music program. With her giving the green light, the creative juices started flowing.

She was a remarkable administrator. It's a rare breed of administrator who will figure out what your strengths are, then let you go with them. I felt able to find my niche and flourish under her.

Source: Reprinted with permission from *Conversations with Great Teachers* by Bill Smoot (2010, 35).

ADMINISTRATORS ARE EVIL, TOO

This is the section I was most reluctant to write.

A good administrator can be really good. A bad administrator can be really, really bad. This might seem like common sense. However, in today's teacher-blaming climate I think this is worth scrutinizing. After all, bad teachers only spoil their own class. A bad administrator can poison an entire school.

Bad administrators aren't necessarily mean-spirited or incompetent. Sometimes you only see their shadow side during contract negotiations. Otherwise helpful principals can be tyrants at the bargaining table, undermining their kindness at school by taking away the wages and benefits that keep good teachers there.

There's not much you can do about a bad administrator—besides having an active union to protect you and the students. (One thing you can do is outlast them, as they often don't stick around too long.) Always ask about the administration before applying to work at a new school. Then again, if the administration is really bad, it'll probably be the first thing you hear about.

Here's the second half of David Lazerson's story about administrators.

Before, I was at a school in another district, and the young assistant principal felt threatened by me because I had been teaching over twenty years and I had a Ph.D. I could care less about that, but he felt threatened. He didn't know a blithering thing about special ed and special needs. So we always butted heads. At one point he said to me, "You are the worst teacher I've ever worked with." I eventually resigned from the school district in order to move on and see what else was out there.

Then this job came along, and it was a godsend. That showed me that sometimes you just have to take risks. My resigning was a big thing; it meant that I was jobless for four or five months. You begin to question yourself. But now I feel like I've died and gone to heaven.

Source: Reprinted with permission from *Conversations with Great Teachers* by Bill Smoot (2010, 35).

LEAVE YOUR JOB (AND GET A BETTER ONE)

They don't deserve you.

It's easiest for new teachers to get their first jobs at a big institution with high turnover due to poor pay and working conditions. That's where the bulk of entry-level jobs are. In other words, you're disconcertingly likely to start somewhere terrible. The reverse is also true. The best jobs are often at small, high-quality institutions where no one ever wants to leave.

Be candid when you appraise your job. If it's a dead end, without the resources to sustain you or opportunities for growth, then it's not good enough for you. Work hard, learn (and give) as much as you can, and get out.

There's so much churn in adult education that many of the people you work with—especially the ambitious—will eventually leave for greener pastures. (This includes administrators.) Keep in touch with them! These are the people most likely to get you your next, better job.

Don't martyr yourself. Don't stay in a bad school any longer that you have to. They need good teachers everywhere.

> **Hint:** *Another good reason to quit a bad school is that they may turn around and fire you for no reason. After all, the inability to recognize good teaching is one of the main things that makes a bad school bad.*

IT'S A SETUP!

If it's too good to be true, it probably is.

You get an amazing new job. The mission is ambitious, the stakes are high, and you can't believe they hired you. Here's the bad news: the job sounds amazing because it's impossible.

People start all sorts of wildly unrealistic projects with the best of intentions, especially in education, because the American narrative of redemption through learning is so powerful. Sadly, unrealistic educational projects are bad for everyone. You, the teacher, feel like garbage because you can't meet your goals, your students' needs don't get met, and an institution based on a flawed premise continues to grow.

A setup like this can be very difficult to recognize while you still don't know what can't be done. It can be perversely harder to recognize if your administrators are kind and supportive. In fact, it happens most often when a school's founders are too idealistic.

Story: I once worked for a nonprofit that provided ESL instruction in the workplace for undocumented janitorial staff. I was excited, but quickly saw that students' progress was extremely slow. After a few frustrating months I realized that our program offered many fewer hours of class time than a traditional adult school—because that's all that the janitorial company would agree to. And since students were paid for the (brief) time they were in class, many showed up with no intention of studying. The organization had an admirable mission that was impossible to fulfill. I left the job shortly thereafter.

GET THE MOST FROM A CONFERENCE

You will get out of it what you put into it.

Conferences are amazing. They're a unique opportunity to see just how broad and how deep your field is, and for meeting future

173

collaborators and employers alike. Having said that, they can also be overwhelming. Here's how you can make the most of any conference you go to.

Before the Conference

In chronological order:

· Apply early for any professional development funds from your school.
· Apply for conference grants, such as a new teacher travel grant, or a first-time attendee grant.
· Make business cards you can give to people you meet, and to enter into drawings.
· Register early to save money!
· Apply to be a volunteer to save on registration and meet people.
· Find cheap or free housing—with friends, at a hostel, or sharing a hotel room.
  · The closer you stay to the conference, the more stuff you can go to, the more people you meet, and the more you get out of the conference overall.
· Read through the whole schedule for the conference:
  · Identify several promising workshops in each time slot, balancing between those based on theory, practice, and demonstrating new products: textbooks, software, and so on.
  · Map out where they're physically happening at the hotel or convention center.
· Look beyond workshops. Check for interest-group meetings, regional groups or caucuses: Women in the Trades, Great Lakes Region, LGBT, and so on.

During the Conference

- Register and note if any workshops you're interested in have been moved or canceled—or if any promising new workshops are being offered.
- Go to the vendors' floor to check out textbooks and collect convention swag: sample textbooks, tote bags, flash drives, and the like. (You get the best stuff at the very beginning and very end.)
- Introduce yourself to everyone! Presenters, the person sitting next to you at a workshop, the person standing behind you in the bathroom line . . . Meeting people is one of the main things you get out of a conference.
- Go to workshops:
  - Collect any handouts as soon as you come in. They often run out, you can quickly see if the workshop is interesting or relevant to you, and they always have the presenters' contact info.
  - Sit in the back and quietly leave if it's not what you want. This is normal conference etiquette and makes space for latecomers.
  - If you do leave early, consult your map of interesting workshops to see what else is happening nearby. You can duck into a bunch this way without losing time running around.
  - If a workshop is good, talk to the presenter(s) at the end and exchange information for follow-up communication or collaboration.
- Take breaks—good conferences are mind-blowing. Go for a walk or even visit a local museum.
- Meet up with any alumni groups you're a part of. Many schedule reunions at conferences.

- Socialize! Go to organized mixers or spontaneous outings with other attendees.
- Keep all your receipts for reimbursement or tax purposes.

After the Conference

- Go through your handouts, keeping the good stuff and recycling the rest.
- E-mail anyone you made a good connection with.
- E-mail everyone you said you'd follow up with. Keep a list for this purpose during the conference.
- Apply exciting new practices you learned about while they're fresh and you're inspired.
- Present anything interesting you learned to your peers.
- Submit an application to present at next year's conference.

CONTRIBUTE TO YOUR FIELD

Practice, publish, present, and post.

A defining quality of experts is that they contribute to their field. I think this is actually more important for teachers who don't teach academic subjects. If you teach poetry, get your poems published. If you teach carpentry, keep working in the shop or at a job site.

Contributing to your field ensures that you're able to meet the professional standards of your peers—as opposed to simply performing better than your students. You also won't become irrelevant by teaching students what they needed to know ten years ago. And you'll enjoy more credibility with students, who know you can do what you ask of them.

Finally, contributing to your field helps you see from the students' perspective. Submitting your work to a journal or a competition is the closest you'll get, in terms of anxiety and fear, to what students experience when they take their final exams. What else is going to get you out of your professional comfort zone?

TEACH WHERE YOU LIVE

Commute time is inversely proportional to happiness.

Living close to school is one of the secrets to a happy teaching career. You get to know the community you serve; you bump into students; you save time on your commute—and money, if you walk or bicycle instead of taking public transit or driving.

There are less obvious benefits, too. Living close to school makes it easier to do those little things that help your career, such as going to staff meetings, checking your school mailbox, participating in professional development, and generally engaging in school outside your classroom.

A 2010 study found a happy marriage and a short commute to be the two biggest factors in people's happiness. It's not always possible to live close to school. But when it is, I suggest you try it.

Story: I'll never forget the first time I walked to the corner grocery store and heard a voice call out, "Teacher! Teacher!" It's still the best feeling in the world. You'll be amazed how many current and former students will be excited to see you—even those who never seemed excited about your class while they were in it.

TEACH WHAT YOU LOVE

At least find something you love about what you teach.

We sometimes teach subjects we don't actually love. Perhaps subjects that no one has ever loved. I spent a year teaching cabinetmaking-related English! The Dalai Lama couldn't love that!

The trick is to find something about your subject that you genuinely appreciate. For all the challenges of the ESL-for-cabinetmakers class, the machines were pretty cool, and I'm now conversant in planers and band saws.

When you teach a subject of any depth there will be something in it that will appeal to you. Take grammar. (Please!) It's one of the most difficult ESL topics to teach. But the challenge of doing so appeals to some teachers. Its rule-bound nature appeals to others. I always liked approaching grammar based on what people actually use in conversation—for example, how the present continuous is used for future actions. ("I am skiing tomorrow.")

Students are perceptive. If you care about your subject, they're more likely to care about it, too. Find at least one thing you genuinely love and go from there.

HAVE AMAZING INSTRUCTION IN YOUR LIFE

Be the student for a change.

Teachers tend to believe that there is one clear standard for good teaching—their own. The better your methods work for you, the more likely you are to keep using them and the harder it will be to learn a new approach, which is going to suck when you have a student (or a class) for whom your approach doesn't work at all.

The best antidote I've found to getting stuck in a teaching rut is having amazing instruction in my own life. I get to see completely different teaching methodologies in my dojo from those I use in my classroom, even if the underlying principles are the same—such as seeing from the student's perspective. I've learned at least as much about teaching by studying martial arts as I did in graduate school.

Amazing instruction is also a good way to stay inspired when teaching gets you down. If nothing else, it's nice to be the student for once, and not have to worry about anyone's learning but your own.

REMEMBER THE HORRIBLE INSTRUCTION IN YOUR LIFE

There are lessons only pain can teach you.

For my master's degree in teaching ESL, I had to spend a semester observing a professor who turned out to be a horrible instructor. It was literally the most painful experience of my life. Literally "literally." (A couple years earlier, I had my collarbone broken by a hit-and-run while biking home from teaching. I would happily sacrifice another fractured clavicle in exchange for not having to observe this teacher again.)

About halfway through the term, I got it. I was put into that class to understand how painful bad instruction is, and to remember to always strive to be a great teacher.

Having understood what the universe had offered me, I quit observing the class a month early. But I probably learned more from that experience than any other in grad school. Come to think of it, that may have been the most powerful learning experience of my entire life.

(Not incidentally, this teacher thought she was amazing. And her students didn't seem to know any better.)

> **Hint:** *In your career you will inevitably have to observe bad teachers. Resist the temptation to mentally check out. Instead, analyze what exactly makes this teacher so ineffective, even sketching out in real time how their class could be improved. Imagine how you might (kindly) talk to them about what's going wrong, even if that's not going to happen. You can learn a lot from observing a bad teacher.*

READ MORE EDUCATION BOOKS

It's like traveling to another country—or another planet.

I know, I know. An author telling you to read more books is like the American Chocolate Association saying your ideal weight is four hundred pounds.[1] But hear me out on this one.

The best part of writing this book has been discovering the many others written on the topic. I found an author who asks big questions about the meaning of education and knowledge (*What Is Education?* by Philip Jackson), a book about the purpose of college (*College* by Andrew Delbanco) and another written specifically for college professors teaching English classes (*The Chicago Handbook for Teachers* by Brinkley et al.).

I've found books about how messed up the adjunct system is and how to fight for something better (*Reclaiming the Ivory Tower: Organizing Adjuncts to Save Higher Education* by Joe Berry). I read a book that was, at least at first glance, so similar to mine that I considered giving up (*Tools for Teaching* by Barbara Davis). I read what I believe to be the best book about adult education ever written (*Facilitating Group Learning* by George Lakey).

I'm a better person for having read these books. Ideally, I'm also a better teacher, too. So despite the fact you're not getting paid enough and receive little to no professional development, I beg you to explore the universe of adult education literature. They'll help you make sense of your students, your practice, and your new professional life.

A teaching book can be a window onto another way of practice or the doorway to Narnia. My bibliography at the end of this book lists not just the works referenced here but all the best education books I've found so far. I envy how many we have still to discover.

Story: One warm summer day, my partner and I went to our favorite sidewalk cafe in Berkeley. As we waited outside for our order, she spied a box of books left out on the sidewalk. While I was still standing around like a dummy, she found in the box an old paperback with a naked bearded man on the cover.

It turned out to be something of a lost classic: *On Learning and Social Change*, by Michael Rossman. It was a collection of essays by a radical educator who came of age during Berkeley's free speech slash antiwar slash anti-establishment heyday in the 1960s. The accounts of his struggle to replace the alienation of the university with peer learning networks was inspiring. His educational experiments in psychedelic drugs were astonishing.

Sometimes a book is letter from a foreign country. *On Learning and Social Change* was a portal to another dimension.

I was shown how cataclysmic things had been just forty
years earlier, how education was central to that cataclysm, and
how much, and how little, things had changed since—all in
Berkeley, the very place my partner found that book for me
on the sidewalk. (That's why we got married. One reason, at
least.)

READ OUTSIDE YOUR FIELD

You will find unexpected connections to your courses.

I believe that reading outside your field is one of the best things
you can do for your teaching practice. For me, reading nonfiction
has been a great way to find connections between my curriculum
and my students. For a while I was on a business reading kick. I
read a typical MBA's first-year book list, including such canonical
works as *Good to Great* and *The Toyota Way*.

A few months later, I was assigned a technical reading
and writing class. My students would be adults coming back to
school to get certified as welders or heating/ventilation/air condi-
tioning (HVAC) technicians. I knew nothing about welding or
HVAC. Then I realized that my business reading had taught me
how modern industry is obsessed with improving its own
processes. (This is *kaizen*, a term for continuous improvement
coined by Toyota and used everywhere commodities are mass
produced.)

I was able to build my course around the assumption that
my students would ultimately get jobs where they would have to
keep abreast of process changes and perhaps even author some of
their own. This helped me answer one of the big questions I

struggled with when designing the course: "Why should my students care about technical reading?"

DEVELOP A NETWORK OF PEERS YOU RESPECT
Avoid the haters.

Adult education teachers have one of the loneliest jobs in America. We're all busy and transient. We teach alone in the classroom. We work intensely with our students, who all leave us by the end of the term. Part-timers are often deprived of any faculty community. And then we don't get rehired and have to start all over again at a new school. (Thanks to Joe Berry's *Reclaiming the Ivory Tower* [2005] for this useful and depressing insight.)

Overcome that isolation by collaborating with your peers. Collaboration will also help you grow as a teacher. This can happen through a formal mentoring process but, I think, is more likely to happen informally. I can't tell you how much I learned while biking home with two of my senior colleagues after my evening class. This was in Oakland, so we started riding together for safety, but it ended up being an education in and of itself.

A group can do more than the sum of its parts. Find other teachers at your school who are effective and with whom you get along. Then find ways to work together, such as serving on committees, developing curriculum, or simply troubleshooting and strategizing over drinks after work.

In my opinion, proximity is key. It's better to collaborate with a good teacher you see all the time than to court a phenomenal teacher you never cross paths with. Find people you like who you see frequently and start working together right away.

Discussed While Biking Home with Don and Barbara

Topics explored on our way from 6th Avenue to 38th Avenue:

- The best school district to teach for
- Easier ways to fill out attendance sheets
- Following up on individual students who had been in our classes
- The deal with the new guy
- Which grammar book to use
- If it was worth going to the regional ESL teacher conference (yes)
- Whether to focus on writing paragraphs at the intermediate level
- Teaching English in Korea
- The merits of a monolingual versus multilingual class
- Celine Dion versus Johnny Cash in the classroom
- Whether to call the police upon seeing a young teenage prostitute (yes)

Hint: One bad apple can F-up your network. Be choosy about who you invite. A good attitude is way more important than being an amazing teacher. There are plenty of teachers who are fantastic in the classroom and have zero social skills with their peers.

MAKE MEETINGS PRODUCTIVE

Follow these steps to have a good meeting every time.

Teachers spend a lot of time in meetings. Whether it's choosing new technology for the classroom or organizing events for students, we all benefit when our meetings go smoothly. The following tips will help you make every meeting you go to be more productive. These tips work best for smaller meetings of folks working together on an ongoing basis, perhaps five to fifteen people on a committee. You'll see that a lot of classroom best practices apply to meetings, too!

○ *Start on time.* Starting late fosters a culture of lateness and punishes those who show up on time.

○ *Check in.* Do a go-round where everyone says a sentence or two about how they're doing. If one or more people are in crisis, it's better to address it right away than let those crises undermine the whole meeting.

○ *Make an agenda with times on it.* Literally every meeting should have an agenda of what's to be discussed and how long to spend on each topic. Review the agenda to make sure you have everything.

○ *Assign roles.* Typical meeting roles are time keeper, minutes taker and facilitator. (The same person can facilitate and keep time.) If there's a contentious decision to make, the facilitator should not be someone deeply invested in that decision.

○ *Take minutes.* Notes or it didn't happen. Just write down what you agreed on and who committed to which tasks; notes should not be a verbatim record of everything said. Send out the notes at the end of the meeting to everyone in the group, including those who couldn't make it.

○ *Stick to the agenda.* A good agenda puts discussion topics in a logical order. Stick to that order. It's tempting to jump to another topic when it comes up, but starting a new discussion when you haven't finished the one at hand will almost always waste a lot of time.

○ *Step up, step back.* Don't let a couple of people dominate conversation. Every group has some members with more experience and more to say, and that's fine. However, there should

185

still be room for everyone to ask questions and explore the best solutions. Part of knowing a lot is knowing when to listen, and knowing not to respond to every single person who speaks.

○ *You can't always make everyone happy.* Most small groups operate by consensus. Consensus means that everyone's concerns are heard and you collectively try to address them. The goal is to come up with the best possible solution, one that everyone is invested in. Consensus is not making everyone happy. Part of being useful in a group is knowing when to accept that you won't get your way this time, stating your dissent, and then going with the decision the rest of the group wants.

○ *Delegate.* Delegate tasks and decision making to individuals or subcommittees whenever possible. For example, if your technology committee needs to find a new blogging service for students, spend just five minutes brainstorming sites. Then the three teachers most interested in the topic can look into those sites and others and e-mail their analysis to the committee members, who will evaluate each one on their own. At the next meeting the committee can discuss their opinions and vote. This is way better than everyone spending an entire meeting clicking through websites.

○ *End by scheduling your next meeting.* People need to know when and where the next meeting is so they're available for it. Try to accommodate folks who couldn't make it to this meeting—say, by making it on a different day of the week, or at another time of the day.

○ *End on time.* It's fine if you choose to go late because you needed a few more minutes to make the best decision possible. But meetings usually go over simply because there was no agenda (with times) to begin with, and folks went off topic. If you follow the rules here your meetings will end on time more often than not, accomplishing everything you needed to.

186

DON'T GO BACK TO SCHOOL UNTIL YOU HAVE TO

Then go back as soon as possible.

You often need a graduate degree to get ahead in teaching. So when do you go back to school for your MA or PhD? Not until you absolutely need to. Grad school is expensive, considering the loans you take out and the lost wages for the years you're in school. Given how short a teaching career can be, you could end up spending more time studying for your degree than using it.

Wait until you know you want to keep teaching. If possible, wait until you need an advanced degree to go from working part-time to full-time, from full-time to tenure, or from teaching to administration. Then go to grad school ASAP. As Harry said to Sally, "When you realize you want to spend the rest of your life [teaching college-level mathematics], you want the rest of your life to start as soon as possible."

Hint: Look at the school you want to work for and see where those teachers got their degrees. Many adult ed institutions hire graduates from local universities that they're familiar with. They may prioritize a degree from a nearby second-tier school over an Ivy League program a thousand miles away.

TAKE ADVANTAGE OF BEING UNEMPLOYED

Call it a "surprise sabbatical."

Bruce Lee developed the martial art style Jeet Kun Do, a combination of kung fu and Lee's own insights. Although he spent years developing and even teaching his art, he didn't document any of it until he was bedridden from a training accident. (In the Bruce Lee biopic *Dragon* he was laid low by an underhanded opponent in a Chinatown duel. That's Hollywood for you.)

Downtime from teaching doesn't mean you can't hone your craft. Indeed, there's a kind of deep reflection and self-study that can only happen outside the day-to-day crush of classroom teaching. That's why the academy created the sabbatical—a break from teaching once every seven years.

Part and parcel with adult education is getting laid off. After you work through being sad and pissed off—rightfully so, in most cases—try to take advantage of your newfound freedom. Better laid off occasionally than stuck in a rut your whole career. This book was started during a year spent writing curriculum, my first year out of the classroom in almost a decade. That's no coincidence.

> **Hint:** *Part-time teachers are often eligible for unemployment, even if they're laid off every summer. Don't take management's word on it—check with your union, a senior teacher, or the unemployment office. (We have teachers' unions to thank for successfully litigating this.)*

EVERYTHING I'VE TOLD YOU IS WRONG

Or, at least, only partially true.

Writing this book was like a graduate program tailored exactly to what I needed—but instead of culminating in a long-winded document no one will ever look at, I've produced something that perhaps dozens of people will end up reading.

But there's one thing I sincerely regret about writing this book. It's the fact that, as the author, I have to sound so authoritative about what I put forth here, perhaps at the expense of all the other forms of teaching you might encounter.

To take just one example, I talk a big game about planning your whole course from the beginning—which I honestly believe is good practice. However, there's amazing instruction based on the teacher organizing things just a step ahead of students doing them. These classes facilitate learning based on exactly what students need in that moment. What they offer is, in some ways, more powerful than a planned class ever could be. But I don't talk about them, because I can't do that myself and therefore have no business trying to teach anyone else to do it.

If you see teaching that's different from what I've described, please give it a chance. And if you teach differently from how I suggest, please don't assume that I think you're full of it. I probably just don't know how to do what you do yet.

NOTES

1. Paraphrased from Louie Anderson, *Mom! Louie's Looking at Me Again!* J2 Communications, 1989.

CHAPTER 10

The Future of Education

WE NEED TO TALK ABOUT EDUCATION

It's simply too important to leave to the experts.

This chapter is my attempt to identify what's wrong with education. I'll start with a perspective born of my frustration, as a teacher and as a student both. I'll end with a vision of just how good education could be. Those of us fighting for social justice focus too much on what we are against. I'm going to articulate exactly what I'm for.

Our enemies know exactly what they want: to replace all public and nonprofit schools with for-profit education businesses; to replace skilled, unionized workers with unskilled laborers; to limit students to studying only what makes them useful to corporations; and to transfer as much money as possible from government and students to investors and CEOs.

The debate over education is the fight for the future itself. But as everyday people, we're not exactly encouraged to take part in this debate. Indeed, experts tell us that unless we understand everything about education we're not allowed to talk about it.

But that's exactly what happened to our economy. Up until 2008, economists told us everything was fine, while banks invented increasingly exotic financial instruments with which to rip us off. The economy crashed because everyday people were excluded from any conversation about the economy.

We all have a stake in our education system. Experts or not, we all need to be part of this conversation.

WHAT IS EDUCATION?

The short answer.

My cynical definition of education is, "The formal system by which a society trains its population to be the kind of people it needs."

That's it. Society shapes people in any number of other ways, too: through mass media, the health care system, the law, and so on. But education is unique in that everyone is expected to go through 12+ years of it for the specific purpose of re-creating society. In exchange, education gives us our best shot at becoming who we want to be.

Any self-respecting teacher would say that they are giving their students their best chance at living happy, wise, and free. I tend to disagree. Let's go.

WHAT THE CRISIS IN EDUCATION IS NOT

It's not an inability to transmit information.

It's common knowledge that there's a crisis in education. The analysis goes like this.

192

1. Test scores show that American students lag behind those in China, Japan, Finland, and so on.
2. This is a crisis.
3. Therefore, we must radically change the education system.

I disagree with the first two points. (I'll come back to the third one later.) The data show that middle-class American students rank fifth in the world in science and math; wealthy students rank third (National Center for Education Statistics, 2009; Taylor, 2010). There's no crisis there. American schools are tops when it comes to transmitting information to students whose basic needs are met.

The test score crisis is actually a crisis of poverty. Even schools that claim to excel at helping poor students fail badly at it. For example, the famed KIPP charter school chain brags about how 95 percent of their students, overwhelmingly at-risk, graduate from KIPP high schools and go to college. But we know that only 40 percent of them graduate from college (KIPP, 2012). Compare that to a 69 percent graduation rate for middle-class students, and a 75 percent rate for students whose families earn $70,000 a year or more (Luhbi, 2011; Council of Independent Colleges, 2012).

KIPP's students struggle so much because they are poor. Poor students are less likely to have healthy meals, medical care, warm clothes, and safe neighborhoods. They change schools more often due to getting evicted or foreclosed upon, or because a parent has to move to find work. They have to quit school early to earn money for their families. The consensus is that socioeconomic status accounts for about 60 percent of student achievement. The students themselves account for another 20 percent. Teachers and schools—including facilities and administrators—account for the last 20 percent of achievement.[1]

Another perspective is the United States' standing in PISA, a test of 15-year-olds around the world in math, science, and reading, conducted by the Organisation for Economic Co-operation and Development (OECD). The OECD found that poor students in the U.S. did significantly worse than poor students in other countries. (Programme for International Student Assessment (PISA) Results from PISA 2012 http://www.oecd.org/pisa/keyfindings/PISA-2012-results-US.pdf)

The OECD chides the United States for spending twice as much on education as the Czech Republic while attaining about the same level of math achievement. But according to another OECD study, the U.S. has twice the child poverty rate as the Czech Republic: 20.6 percent here versus 10.3 percent there. (http://stats.oecd.org/Index.aspx?DataSetCode=CWB)

While some developed countries come close, on paper, to our child poverty rate (Germany at 16.3 percent), I think that underestimates the deleterious effects of growing up poor in in the U.S. Because health care is so dependent on income here, and because there is so much violence in poor communities, poor children here suffer more than poor kids in other countries.

It's an ugly fact no one in power wants to admit. As long as there is poverty, students will fail. The effects are so bad that KIPP actually brags about their 60 percent college failure rate. At no point does KIPP, or any other media-recognized education reformer, advocate for fighting poverty first. The only solutions given air time involve destroying teachers' unions and giving more money to corporations—for example, the $468 million the state of Texas is giving to Pearson for a five-year assessment evaluation contract (Schools Matter, 2012). It's a familiar formula in American politics. Any time there's a crisis, private businesses get billions in public money.

American schools are among the best in the world when it comes to educating middle-class kids. So if the crisis in education isn't our inability to transmit information, what is it?

ALIENATION IN EDUCATION

"I'm 39 years old and I still wake up every morning so excited that I don't have to go to school."

—Sarah Silverman, Comedian (2010)

I recently created ESL curriculum on the topic of American high schools. I included an "It Gets Better" video, from the project where thousands of celebrities and everyday people made videos explaining that no matter how bad high school was, particularly for bullied queer youth contemplating suicide, life would get better.

The video I ultimately chose was by Adam Levine, singer for Maroon 5. He said it best: "High school fucking sucked." (He said other things, too.) Levine was referring specifically to the cruelty of his peers, but I have to think it included how unpleasant almost everything about our education system is.

What Makes School Suck?

Here a few things that I think make school suck. Students:

- Are thrown together with hundreds (or thousands) of strangers who immediately form cliques based on superficial differences in background or interests.
- Must study things they know aren't important, which they'll forget about immediately.
- Are subjected to high-stakes tests that focus on rote memorization of facts and procedures.
- Have to wake up early for classes and stay up late doing homework.
- Are herded through an industrial setting like so much human cattle.

195

The common factor that jumps out at me is alienation—forcible separation from your peers, your body, and your interests.

Students are alienated from their peers by having to compete with one another. This happens through academic rankings and the everyday rituals of acting like a good student in class, such as raising your hand and speaking more often than the person sitting next to you. A class may have group activities, but they occur within a context of constant competition. (And you never get to choose who your classmates are.)

Students are alienated from their own bodies by having to sit at a desk all day long. The body's needs are compartmentalized to bathroom breaks, water fountains, vending machines, and persistent fantasies of being anywhere else in the world but in an ugly school building.

Students are finally alienated from their interests—which, in an academic context, are supposed to define who they are—by having to choose between a narrow range of classes within a tiny number of academically recognized disciplines. To add insult to injury, students must engage in any topic the academic way. Consider being forced to write two short stories over three months because "Short Story Writing" was the only English class that appealed to you, when what you really wanted to do was create a high-concept/low-budget science fiction puppet show to put on YouTube. Having to take a class because it's the only one even tangentially related to your passion, or because it fits into your schedule, or because you need it to graduate, is a kind of degradation. It's a perversion of our natural human aptitude for pursuing what excites us.

After years of this alienation you internalize the values of the system you hate. You come to believe that you need an outside authority to tell you what's worth learning—and that any original ideas you have are, by their omission from the official curriculum, worthless. It's believing that even if you did pursue your authentic interests you wouldn't be able to learn anything without all the school BS—credits, semesters, exams—that you hate so much. You are alienated, finally, from any hope of escaping your alienation.

To paraphrase Adam Levine, school sucks. Which leads me to the fundamental contradiction in education today. Why do people love teachers when they hate school so much?

TEACHERS HUMANIZE EDUCATION

That's not necessarily a good thing.

Education is the formal system by which a society trains its population to be the kind of people it needs. That means that the education system looks at an individual student the way the McDonald's restaurant corporation looks at an individual chicken. Education exists to turn a unique human being into another marginal unit of productive society. It turns people into so many student McNuggets.

The process is necessarily alienating. Society's need for obedient citizens is fundamentally at odds with those citizens' needs. If students controlled their own education, after all, they might later expect to control their workplaces, too. That's why our education system is so alienating. The status quo can no more let students design their own schooling than McDonald's could let chickens vote on what happens to them.

So what role do teachers play in all this? We keep students from dropping out of the education process, no matter how bad it gets. How many times have we heard stories of students who had given up all hope until they met the teacher who believed in them? The students who didn't know they could read, or write, or do calculus, until they met the teacher who would change their lives forever?

197

These stories are supposed to be inspiring. I find them depressing. The students in those stories wouldn't have needed a teacher to turn everything around for them if their lives had been going in the right direction in the first place. Can teachers help individual students? Sure. But there is an unsavory role that teachers—especially good ones—play in our schools.

Let me provide an illustration from a "Know Your Rights" training I've given to hundreds of activists around the country. The climax is an interrogation role play where the two trainers role-play being cops while a volunteer from the audience role-plays being an arrestee. The volunteer gets handcuffed and seated in an imaginary interrogation room between the two cops, in front of the audience. The scene begins with the arrestee wisely invoking her Fifth and Sixth Amendment rights by saying, "I'm going to remain silent. I want to see a lawyer."

The first cop, a sergeant, screams at the arrestee about how, if she doesn't talk, she's going to spend years in prison—if the sergeant doesn't beat her up first. The arrestee is shaken but continues to invoke her rights.

At this point the second cop (who we make sure is the same race, gender, and approximate age of the arrestee) asks the sergeant to leave the interrogation room for a few minutes. The second cop then uncuffs the arrestee and says that they know the arrestee's a good kid. However, the sergeant is crazy, and what's worse, the sergeant's uncle is a judge who will put the arrestee in prison for a long time.

But there is a bright side. If the arrestee answers just a few standard questions about the events leading up to the arrest, the second cop will make sure she gets home tonight with no charges.

At this point the sergeant bursts back in and asks the second cop if the arrestee will play ball. The arrestee reluctantly agrees to answer the sergeant's questions. Then the sergeant and the cop step outside the interrogation room and high five. Scene.

198

Anyone familiar with *Law and Order* will recognize this tactic. When we debrief the role play, the "arrestee" invariably says she felt isolated, scared, and powerless. She goes along with the second cop because she psychologically needs a friend, and that cop is her only friend. The tactic is obvious to anyone watching. But cops still use it because it works.

I hope you see where I'm going with this. Our education system is a massive game of good cop/bad cop. The school, in all its alienating power, is the bad cop, coercing its (metaphorically) shackled students. The teacher is the good cop. We tell students that we're looking out for them and how, if they go along with us, we'll make sure they get out of this whole mess.

Obviously, we have better intentions than the "good cop" in the role play, who just wants to make arrestees waive their rights, incriminate themselves, and go to prison. But the effect is the same. Our kindness oils the cogs of the McNugget machine.

We all deserve a higher form of education. Allow me to outline what that might look like.

HOW TO FIX EDUCATION

In two easy steps.

The American education system has failed, but not the way people think it has. As noted, the system is perfectly capable of transmitting information to middle-class students. The problem is that it deliberately alienates students to prepare them for an alienating life. What we need is an education system based on student engagement, to prepare them for a society based on active participation.

I propose that we transform education in two ways. The first is to redesign every academic discipline with the assumption that we are preparing students to be their own teachers. Students should be taught why teachers (and schools) choose the text-books, homework problems, and grading systems that they use. In so doing we can deliberately cultivate students' ability to understand, and then take control of, their own learning.

(Not incidentally, as teachers, we become more thoughtful in choosing our textbooks, homework problems, and grading systems when students are able to critically evaluate our choices.)

As students advance in age and expertise they will be responsible for more and more of their own learning—and each other's learning. They will create their own handouts and lectures: alone, with the teacher, with their classmates, and online with other students. Students will be trained to evaluate and grade each other's assignments and projects. By the time they finish their formal schooling they will be able to teach themselves.

Whew! That was the easy part.

Next, we must transform the education system to make it normal for adults to keep learning in an organized fashion outside of school. After all, everybody knows college and grad school cost too much money, waste too much time, and don't teach what students need in the real world.

I happen to disagree with a lot of those criticisms, but you shouldn't have to go back to school to keep learning. Many people don't have the time, money, or inclination for a college or graduate degree. But all of us need to keep learning, to pay the rent, sure, but more importantly because learning is part of being human, and pursuing what interests us—even just finding out what it is that interests us—is central to a life worth living.

Education should be something that adults keep doing for a lifetime. We must create the structures to facilitate this. This includes making classrooms, machine shops, and laboratories available to independent learners; creating websites to facilitate learner collaboration; and to arrange for experts to help evaluate learners' projects.

Perhaps most important is creating a cultural shift. There must be the expectation that all adults will keep learning, growing, and contributing to human knowledge for their whole lives. Continuing to learn in an organized fashion should be like going to church for Texans, or riding a bicycle for hipsters.

This is an incredibly ambitious project. It could be for the twenty-first century what compulsory public schooling was for the twentieth. So what's the role of teachers in a system based on self-guided learners?

TEACHERS IN A LEARNER-CENTERED WORLD
A future case study.

Let me start with an often unstated point: learning is hard. And if it's hard to learn in school, it's even harder to learn on your own.

Teachers serve a valuable function in the learning process. Teachers know which material to present to students. Teachers know different ways to present important ideas and concepts. Teachers know which errors to correct, and when. Teachers show how their subject is important to the world and relevant to the students, which is part of encouraging students to do their best. Finally, teachers cultivate an environment where students help maximize each other's learning as well as their own. (See? I don't hate teachers.)

Learning in school can be difficult under the best of circumstances. It's hard for most of us to learn calculus, even with good textbooks, engaged peers, and excellent instruction. It's harder still to learn calculus all by yourself.

That's not to say that people never learn outside of school. Self-directed learning happens every day, among "unschooled" children, college students doing independent studies, and working people conducting their own professional development.

201

But teachers still have a vital role to play. Even if students are trained to teach themselves, there will always be areas of study, or times in their lives (cramming for a new job, after the birth of a child, or while caring for an aging parent), when they need a good teacher.

In this world, teachers have transitioned away from being the sole authority in the classroom—from being a benevolent dictator to something closer to a facilitator.

In this model, students are engaged with their peers, their bodies (no more waking up at 7 a.m. to get a parking spot at school!), and with their true interests. Teachers are guides instead of "good cops" because students aren't trapped in an educational jail cell.

This is in stark contrast to both the status quo and the various privatized dystopias that are being proposed today.

Case Study: The Calculus Study Group

The setting: Oakland, California, in the near future.

A group of eight friends want to study calculus together, because they were liberal arts majors who never studied math, but like the idea of learning it. They set aside Tuesday nights for the next eight weeks to come together and study calculus.

They log into a website that's a private-public partnership between government, teachers, business, and students. It's like Facebook meets Yelp meets MIT. The eight friends register their study group. They pay a nominal fee to help cover costs and create buy-in for the course; their workplaces also make a tax-deductible contribution. Finally, the friends take an automated needs assessment that determines their baseline math level and their interests in learning calculus.

The following Tuesday night the eight friends have their first study group and meet their teacher, who appears by video over the Internet. Everyone introduces themselves and the class gets started. The teacher gives a few short lectures along with some problem sets, and the friends variously work individually or as a group to solve them. The night ends with the teacher recommending some resources for further study, a link to a story about how the engineers who built the nearby Golden Gate Bridge used calculus to solve some tricky problems, and some homework based on those problems.

During the second week's study group the teacher recommends learning goals for the class. Based on their interests in local history and the environment, their learning objective for the eight-week course is to measure the impact of solar energy in Oakland. The students decide, in negotiation with the teacher (over difficulty and relevancy to calculus) to estimate how much money would have been saved, if any, had Oakland invested in municipal solar in 1990, using real weather data from that time until today.

Over the eight-week course, the friends are mostly teaching themselves and each other. Each Tuesday night they discuss their calculus studies together, go over the homework, and resolve anything they disagree on. The teacher is there to clarify confusing points and make sure students don't plow forward with incorrect assumptions. The teacher's presence also increases accountability—learners are less likely to blow off their friends and a teacher to watch a ball game. (It helps that the Oakland A's are having a terrible season.)

By week four, it's time for the friends to start hashing out their final project. The teacher provides them with relevant readings and gets them in touch with an expert in industry who can answer their solar questions. The teacher also makes sure enough parameters are covered that the document they produce will be meaningful.

By the end of week eight, the friends have produced a report that, though basic, is useful for other students of calculus, and to their fellow Oakland residents. The teacher checks it for accuracy and completeness. The report helps solidify their learning and gets mentioned in a local news story. Their colleagues see it online and give them props.

After the eight weeks are over, the students take a follow-up exam to measure their math improvement. Once that's completed, their project gets posted to their official online portfolio, where they can show it off to future employers. They also anonymously evaluate their teacher and each other. These rankings give valuable feedback to their peers and the instructor, and help future students choose the teacher best suited for them.

With this case study as a model, we could easily imagine a class of ten different people around the country who learn video production by having a teacher help them choose roles in creating a short documentary—which they ultimately show in a film festival. We could imagine a comp lit class where sisx New Yorkers interpret fiction about British Indians, and six British Indians interpret fiction about New York, and the teacher, a professional writer, helps them organize a discussion between the whole class and one of the authors they read, from which students create a study guide to that author's book.

IT'S TIME TO GO ON THE OFFENSE

The future is unwritten.

We all want to save education. Sadly, we don't have much specific to ask for. Because the political left in this country has failed to provide a vision of what education is supposed to be, we hope, at best, to go back to a time when schools were less underfunded.

We fight for bond measures to offset school budget cuts. We fight against (more) high-stakes testing. By staying on the defense like this, we win most of our battles while losing the war. It doesn't help that the Democratic party mostly supports our opponents' vision of a privatized education system.

There is an overall strategic failure here. By defending the status quo, we're asking Americans to support an education system they probably mostly hated. I have to hand it to our enemies. They're able to use our collective memory of 12+ years of alienation to make any alternative they propose sound good, even if that alternative amounts to watching recorded lectures in front of a computer screen. (Khan Academy, I'm looking at you!)

As an activist, I've learned that you have to go on the offense to win. The first step is to define a future so irresistible that you win from the beginning, at least in the minds of your supporters. If we want to win the fight for education we must begin with our own positive vision of what education should be.

My Definition of "Education."

Here is my vision of an ideal education system:

Education is an ongoing process that helps us understand ourselves and the world. Its aim is to help us become the people we want to be, so that we can create the world we want to live in. Education is a collective enterprise that comes from an unbroken line of students and teachers before us, and exists to benefit everyone alive and everyone who will ever live.

A holistic, ambitious definition of education helps us articulate what we're for and against. Tests that evaluate students according to arbitrary standards? We're against that.

205

Collaboration between teachers and students, and between students all around the world? We're for that.

If you believe in a society where people can collectively solve problems on a local to global scale—not least of which is the problem of how to live a good life while saving the planet—I think you always have to keep the ultimate purpose of education in mind. Education should be a deliberate process over which students have conscious control, not something dictated to them from academia or government or corporations. Nor should it be mediated exclusively through well-intentioned teachers.

Education is, finally, a contradiction. Education belongs to all of us. But for some of us it's a lifetime vocation and for others it is a process to get through as quickly as possible. There will always be a tension between teachers who spend countless hours finding the best ways to help students learn and the students who are supposed to be benefiting from our work. Who decides how classes are taught? Which methods are most effective?

No one has all the answers. But I believe that the best work we do comes from trying to answer those questions that most concern us.

What do you think education is for?

NOTES

1. Nye, B., Konstantopoulos, S., and Hedges, L. V. "How Large Are Teacher Effects?" *Educational Evaluation and Policy Analysis* 26, no. 3 (Fall 2004): 237–257. This paper includes a review of seven previous studies over forty years which show a teacher effect of between 7 and 21 percent on student achievement (239).

Teacher Glossary

Following are the terms you need to know to be an educational professional.

Adjunct: According to Merriam-Webster, "something joined or added to another thing but not essentially a part of it." Ouch. In academic terms, a part-time instructor who receives few to no benefits and has no guarantee of employment. Or, as an administrator tells an adjunct in Joe Berry's *Reclaiming the Ivory Tower,* "You are units of flexibility" (2005, x).

Andragogy: The newer academic term for the practice of teaching adults, as theorized by Malcolm Knowles in 1968. Less frequently used than *Pedagogy.*

Assessment: A test. See *Formative Assessment* and *Summative Assessment.*

Authentic: Real-world materials and tasks not designed or altered for the classroom. Authenticity is like feedback—everybody wants it, but only the right kind and not too much. Finding good authentic materials and tasks is difficult but useful.

Blended Learning: A combination of traditional, in-class instruction, and online instruction.

Classroom Management: The ability to minimize disruptive student behavior and keep the class on track.

Contract: A binding legal agreement that states the rights and responsibilities of the employer and the employee. A teaching contract may never violate state and federal law, including labor law and the educational code ("Ed Code").

Critical Thinking: The ability to go beyond understanding new information to evaluating it from a metalevel. Why do I believe this? Why is this important? What does it take for granted? What questions does it raise? Who does it serve?

Curriculum: The plan for a course or educational program, including the instructional materials students will read, the activities students will do, and the lesson plans the teacher will use.

Formative Assessment: A survey, formal or informal, that asks students their opinion of the class.

Hidden Curriculum: The idea that certain values, especially those benefiting the status quo, are implicitly taught in school. For example, a common criticism of early adult ESL curriculum is that it taught students to correctly take orders from native English speakers without teaching them how to negotiate or refuse them.

Intrinsic-Extrinsic Motivation: Intrinsic motivation comes from within (love of learning, respect for the subject), whereas extrinsic motivation comes from without (getting a raise). Many adult students go to class for the latter, but some of the best learning comes from the former.

Just Cause: A clause in the contract which obligates the administration to have "just cause" (a good reason) to fire, or not rehire, a teacher.

Learning: What happens in the student's head. This is the student's acquisition of new knowledge, understanding, and skills, which takes place in a classroom environment, with peers, or individually. Note that this is related to, but distinct from, *Teaching.*

Learning Objectives or Learning Outcomes: What students should be able to do by the end of an activity, class, or course. Ideally, students will be able to demonstrate their achievement of a learning objective through successfully accomplishing a concrete activity.

Metacognition: Aka "Thinking about thinking." Consciously scrutinizing how you mentally engage a subject. ("Why do I believe handguns are bad? Where have I gotten my information? How much of my opinion is emotional?") This is all the rage in education these days.

Pedagogy (PEH-da-GO-jee): This used to be the generic name for the practice/field of teaching, but now is often used specifically for teaching children.

Professional Development: The process by which professionals continue to learn outside formal educational institutions. This can happen in the workplace, at conferences, or online. Professional development classes and workshops may be led by academics, consultants, or other working professionals.

Realia (REE-al-EE-uh): Physical items for students to look at and engage with in learning. Realia for teaching food vocabulary would be (real or plastic) apples and oranges. Also known as "props."

Standards: The degree to which students must be able to perform the skills they have learned in your class. Standards are the primary way your teaching success is measured.

Strike: When workers collectively withhold their labor. In the movies this is a spontaneous act of defiance or a fight to the finish. In real life, labor law demands that strikes only happen after a "cooling-off" period following failed contract bargaining. (It's almost impossible to strike while the iron is hot—to management's benefit.) In practice, teachers are more likely to have symbolic one- or two-day strikes rather than a last-man-standing type conflict.

Summative Assessment: A test of student achievement of a class's learning objectives.

Syllabus: The document students receive at the beginning of the term which outlines the details of the class: the course description, what students need to bring, how they are expected to participate, what they will learn, and how they'll be evaluated, among other things.

Teaching: What the teacher does. It's the practice of effectively presenting information, structuring activities, choosing assessments, and making corrections, all with the goal of maximizing student learning.

Tenure: A guaranteed full-time teaching or teaching/research position for life, with the right to due process before being fired.

Transfer: The ability to apply knowledge obtained in class out in the real world.

REFERENCES

Arden, P. 2003. *It's Not How Good You Are, It's How Good You Want to Be: The Bestselling Book by Paul Arden*. London: Phaidon Press.

Arden, P. 2006. *Whatever You Think, Think the Opposite*. New York: Portfolio.

Bain, K. 2004. *What the Best College Teachers Do*. Cambridge, MA: Harvard University Press.

Berger, R. 2003. *An Ethic of Excellence: Building a Culture of Craftsmanship with Students*. Portsmouth, NH: Heinemann.

Berry, J. 2005. *Reclaiming the Ivory Tower: Organizing Adjuncts to Save Higher Education*. New York: Monthly Review Press.

Berry, J. 2009. *The Manual of Detection*. New York: Penguin.

Brinkley, A., E. E. El-Fakahany, B. Dessants, M. Flamm, C. B. Forcey Jr., M. L. Ouellette, and E. Rothschild. 2011. *The Chicago Handbook for Teachers: A Practical Guide to the College Classroom*. Chicago: University of Chicago Press.

Brookfield, S. 2013. *Powerful Techniques for Teaching Adults*. San Francisco: Jossey-Bass.

Council of Independent Colleges. July 2012. "Graduation Rates by Family Income." http://www.cic.edu/Research-and-Data/Making-the-Case/Pages/Graduation-Rates-by-Family-Income.aspx

Covey, S. R. 1989. *The Seven Habits of Highly Effective People*. New York: Free Press.

Daloz, L. 2012. *Mentor*. San Francisco: Jossey-Bass.

Davis, B. 2009. *Tools for Teaching*. San Francisco: Jossey-Bass.

Delbanco, A. 2012. *College: What It Was, Is, and Should Be*. Princeton, NJ: Princeton University Press.

Dewey, J. 1938/1997. *Experience & Education*. New York: Touchstone. (Originally published 1938.)

Fight Club. Directed by David Fincher. United States: Fox 2000 Pictures, 1999.

Friend, E. 1957. *Integrated in All Respects*. New Market, TN: Highlander Folk School.

Horton, M. 1998. *The Long Haul*. New York: Teachers College.

Kahn-Russell, J. 2012. "Praxis Makes Perfect." In *Beautiful Trouble*, edited by A. Boyd, 162–163. San Francisco: OR Press.

KIPP. Fall 2012. "Student Attainment." http://www.kipp.org/about-kipp/students

Lakey, G. 2010. *Facilitating Group Learning: Strategies for Success with Adult Learners*. San Francisco: Jossey-Bass.

Lemov, D. 2010. *Teach Like a Champion: 49 Techniques that Put Students on the Path to College*. San Francisco: Jossey-Bass.

Luhbi, T. Nov. 2011. "College Graduation Rates: Income Really Matters." CNNMoney. http://money.cnn.com/2011/11/21/news/economy/income_college/index.htm

Merriam, S. B., R. S. Caffarella, and L. M. Baumgartner. 2007. *Learning in Adulthood: A Comprehensive Guide*. San Francisco: Jossey-Bass.

National Center for Education Statistics. 2009. "U.S. Performance Across International Assessments of Student Achievement: How Much Does Performance Within the United States Vary by School Poverty?" http://nces.ed.gov/programs/coe/analysis/2009-sb3.asp

Schools Matter. May 2012. "Texas Pays Pearson $468,000,000 for 5 Year Contract." http://www.schoolsmatter.info/2012/05/texas-pays-pearson-468000000-for-5-year.html

Silverman, S. Feb. 2010. "A New Perspective on the Number 3000." Lecture, TED Talks, Long Beach, CA.

Smoot, B. 2010. *Conversations with Great Teachers*. Bloomington: Indiana Press.

Stanford, Peter. 2007. *C. Day-Lewis: A Life*. New York City: Continuum.

Sting. 1980. "Don't Stand So Close to Me." The Police, *Zenyatta Mondatta*. A&M AMLH 64831, vinyl LP.

Taylor, J. Dec. 2010. "Are Public Education Chicken Littles Wrong?" http://blog.seattlepi.com/jimtaylor/2010/12/20/are-public -education-chicken-littles-wrong/

Thoreau, H. D. *Walden*. 1854/2013. United States: Empire Books. (Originally published 1854.)

Von Land, J. 1983. *Eichmann Interrogated*. New York: Farrar, Straus, and Giroux.

Zinn, H., and A. Arnove. 2009. *Voices of a People's History of the United States*. New York: Seven Stories Press.

FURTHER READING

Adams, F., and Horton, M. *Unearthing Seeds of Fire: The Idea of Highlander*. Winston-Salem, NC: John F. Blair Publisher, 1975.

> An engaging account of the forging of the Highlander Center, perhaps the most important school in American history. Going back to 1937, Highlander taught generations of union organizers and civil rights activists; it's where the former taught the latter "We Shall Not Be Moved." One of Highlander's founders was Myles Horton, whose amazing stories of organizing, studying, and ultimately teaching in the Tennessee mountains hold this book together. A must-read for anyone who believes in teaching for social justice.

Arden, P. *It's Not How Good You Are, It's How Good You Want to Be: The Bestselling Book by Paul Arden*. London: Phaidon Press, 2003.

> A triple shot of espresso in paperback, *It's Not How Good You Are* is an entertaining and even enlightening manifesto on the relationship between creativity, fulfillment, and profit by one of the greatest admen of all time. Reading it will immediately inspire you to be the best teacher in the world. (The illustrations are fun, too.)

Bain, K. *What the Best College Teachers Do*. Cambridge, MA: Harvard University Press, 2004.

> A collection of best practices from accomplished college teachers around the country. Ken Bain convinced me of the importance of syllabuses and making final exams cumulative, among many other things.

Berger, R. *An Ethic of Excellence: Building a Culture of Craftsmanship with Students*. Portsmouth, NH: Heinemann, 2003.

> Living in a town so small "even other people in the state have never heard of it" (p. 13), Ron Berger and his five fellow

elementary school teachers created an entire school culture that cultivated excellence. From kindergarten, children promote to the next grade by presenting a portfolio of their work to a panel of teachers and townspeople. Although the book's focus is on children, the ideas around building a culture of excellence apply just as much to adults. And it's a wonderful, short read. Another magic find from the Strand bookstore in New York.

Berry, J. *Reclaiming the Ivory Tower: Organizing Adjuncts to Save Higher Education.* New York: Monthly Review Press, 2005.

An excellent and depressing account of the sorry state of non-tenured teachers today. Joe Berry convincingly explains what is wrong with schools' increasing reliance on adjunct teachers ("units of flexibility," as one administrator memorably puts it) and gives steps on how we can organize for better.

Brinkley, A., El-Fakahany, E. E., Dessants, B., Flamm, M., Forcey, C. B. Jr., Ouellette, M. L., and Rothschild, E. *The Chicago Handbook for Teachers: A Practical Guide to the College Classroom.* Chicago: University of Chicago Press, 2011.

A useful guide for beginning university teachers, the *Chicago Handbook* has lucid explanations of how to lead classroom discussions, deliver lectures, and write an effective syllabus, among many other things. Though they have an admitted bias toward university English classes, it contains good information for any kind of teaching.

Brookfield, S. *Powerful Techniques for Teaching Adults.* San Francisco: Jossey-Bass, 2013.

Stephen Brookfield may be the best-known adult education author today. In *Powerful Techniques,* he grapples with how power permeates the university classroom, whether we acknowledge it or not, in ways detrimental to both students and teachers alike. While I am quicker to acknowledge the positive effects of power differentials—like the fact that I don't have to lesson plan!—this book was eye opening and thought provoking. A fine introduction to Brookfield's work.

Daloz, L. *Mentor.* San Francisco: Jossey-Bass, 2012.

While providing a survey of several major theories of adult development, Daloz uses the metaphor of a journey to describe the paths that adult learners take. Along the way he explains what holds them back and how we can help them grow. Daloz's beautiful descriptions of both the learning process and the state of Vermont, where much of the book takes place, make reading *Mentor* a pleasure.

Davis, B. *Tools for Teaching*. San Francisco: Jossey-Bass, 2009.

Tools is a comprehensive guide to the many challenges that higher education instructors face. If you teach at a college or university and want a manual that covers more topics and techniques than mine—without the anecdotes—*Tools for Teaching* is the place to go.

Delbanco, A. *College: What It Was, Is, and Should Be*. Princeton, NJ: Princeton University Press, 2012.

The ancient Greeks had a system where young men in their late teens to early twenties lived, studied, and played sports together. This is just one happy surprise in Delbanco's wonderful book that puts college—an institution focused on instruction, as opposed to the university, which is dedicated to creating new knowledge—in a historical context, and explains why it's needed now as much as ever.

Dewey, J. *Experience & Education*. New York: Touchstone, 1997. (Originally published 1938.)

John Dewey is the granddaddy of American education theory. A public intellectual, he founded a school where he experimented with the then-radical notion that children were not blank tablets for old information to be imprinted upon via rote memorization and drills, but sentient beings who needed to construct meaning on their own, in no small part to be able to learn new ideas in the future. This thin book is considered perhaps the best distillation of his beliefs.

Freire, P. *Pedagogy of the Oppressed*. New York: Continuum, 1970.

The most overrated book in education. Paulo Freire's turgid prose belabors many ideas that Myles Horton had put into action decades before. However, because of their institutional bias, ed departments around the United States celebrate the work of this professor over Horton, an educator who worked outside the academy.

You should be conversant in Freire because he's such a well-known name. (He has some good ideas, too.) I suggest bell hooks's *Teaching to Transgress,* which summarizes and supplements *Pedagogy.* Another option is *We Make the Road by Walking,* a transcript of a lively conversation between Myles Horton and Paulo Freire.

Greive, D. *A Handbook for Adjunct/Part-Time Faculty and Teachers of Adults.* Ann Arbor, MI: Part-Time Press, 2011.

The thin book on how to teach adults. Dr. Greive provides a fabulous introduction to preparing your college class, delivering your lessons, and evaluating your students.

Jackson, P. *What Is Education?* Chicago: University of Chicago Press, 2011.

A beautiful, trim hardcover that engages its titular question in unabashedly philosophical terms. What is education? What is truth? Philip Jackson is unafraid to begin well past where other teaching books end. I thought I knew exactly what education was. Now I know I'll be answering this question for at least as long as the author has.

Kahn-Russell, J. "Praxis Makes Perfect." *In Beautiful Trouble.* Edited by A. Boyd. San Francisco: OR Press, 2012.

A tidy little essay by Joshua Kahn-Russell about the importance of theory and reflection—even when we're tempted to simply act for the sake of doing something. While he's talking about organizing for social justice, the praxis wheel is of use when doing anything that matters.

Klein, G. *Sources of Power: How People Make Decisions.* Cambridge, MA: MIT Press, 1999.

Through quirky but thorough research methodologies, Gary Klein and his team of researchers explain how experts make good decisions under pressure. In a nutshell, experts' depth of knowledge lets them compare the unique crisis before them to the myriad ones they've encountered before. They can immediately identify the most crucial factors at play, speculate (correctly) on their origin, and imagine possible outcomes. Klein makes a convincing case that alongside experience, the power of imagination is something that sets experts apart from the rest of us. An invaluable book for anyone who aspires to be an expert.

Lakey, G. *Facilitating Group Learning: Strategies for Success with Adult Learners*. San Francisco: Jossey-Bass, 2010.

Not just the best book on teaching I've ever read, but perhaps just the best book I've read, period. Lakey has spent his life helping people organize for social justice, often through his workshops and trainings with the outstanding group Training for Change. Combining accessible theory, concrete suggestions, and amazing stories from his career as an educator, Lakey gives you a book made of wisdom.

Lemov, D. *Teach Like a Champion: 49 Techniques That Put Students on the Path to College*. San Francisco: Jossey-Bass, 2010.

Doug Lemov urgently makes the case for applying best teaching practices in the classroom. Despite its K–12 focus, *Champion* names and explains a number of techniques you'll be able to use in your classroom tomorrow. You won't be able to put it down.

Merriam, S. B., Caffarella, R. S., and Baumgartner, L. M. *Learning in Adulthood: A Comprehensive Guide*. San Francisco: Jossey-Bass, 2007.

This is the only book of adult educational theory you need to read. That's because it covers seemingly every topic in adult education. Merriam et al. do a great job of summarizing the histories and great debates in our field, boiling everything down to comprehensible chunks.

Renner, P. *The Art of Teaching Adults: How to Become an Exceptional Instructor & Facilitator*. Vancouver, BC: Training Associates, 1993.

Peter Renner focuses on the nuts and bolts of creating and leading workshops. He breaks down how to facilitate discussions, take notes on the board, and many of the other concrete teaching skills.

Rossman, M. *On Learning and Social Change*. New York: Random House, 1972.

The naked screaming man in lotus position on the cover tells you this is no ordinary education book. Michael Rossman was a traveling adjunct, education consultant, and organizer for social change during the late 1960s through mid-1970s. His essays range from deprogramming square college students using radical education to big-picture analyses of education and society. Though some of the writing feels dated, the introductory chapter, where he shows how acting like a good student actually inhibits learning, is worth the price of entry. A true lost classic.

Saphier, J., and Gower, R. *The Skillful Teacher: Building Your Teaching Skills.* Acton, MA: Research for Better Teaching, 2008.

Simply the most comprehensive book on the skills that constitute good teaching. Though it focuses on K–12 education, there's a lot here for teachers of adults to use. Perhaps most fascinating is the chapter "Principles of Learning," with twenty-four skills that don't fit under any other category. At close to six hundred pages, I wouldn't make this your first teaching book to read cover to cover, but it's invaluable as a reference.

Smoot, B. *Conversations with Great Teachers.* Bloomington: Indiana Press, 2010.

The book that inspired this one. Smoot interviewed a middle school special education teacher, a master farrier (horseshoe maker), a yoga instructor who teaches women in prison, a politics professor who teaches newly elected congressional representatives, and many more great teachers around the country. Each one has something important to offer us. Studs Terkel meets Jonathan Kozol. Totally engrossing.

Stigler, J. W., and Hiebert, J. *The Teaching Gap.* New York: Free Press, 2009.

The rare book that changes your understanding of the field. *The Teaching Gap* is ostensibly about an international study of classroom teaching in the United States, Germany, and Japan. However, the authors focus on their most powerful finding: that Japanese schools are highly effective due to "Lesson Study," where teachers at almost every elementary school in the country collaborate on individual lessons, teach them, evaluate them, change them, and teach (and evaluate) them again, and then submit their findings and lessons to the national government, which may implement their changes at schools around the country.

The authors make a convincing case that this ongoing process, one which makes teachers into researchers, is responsible for fifty years of incremental improvement in Japanese teaching, and has made Japanese math classes (the focus of the study) among the best in the world. Contrast that to America's quick-fix culture of education reform.

INDEX

If you enjoyed this book, you may also like these:

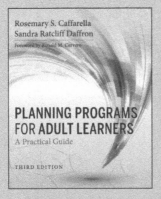

Planning Programs for Adult Learners, 3rd ed.
by Rosemary S. Caffarella, Sandra Ratcliff Daffron
ISBN: 9780470770375

Tools for Teaching, 2nd ed.
by Barbara Gross Davis
ISBN: 9780787965679

Powerful Techniques for Teaching Adults
by Stephen D. Brookfield
ISBN: 9781118017005

Student Engagement Techniques
by Elizabeth F. Barkley
ISBN: 9780470281918